Pie in the Sky Adventures

Don and Teri Murray

Edited by Sarah Williams

Cover Art by Tina Rose

Copyright © 2013 Don and Teri Murray

All rights reserved.

ISBN-10:1492955116
ISBN-13: 9781492955115

DEDICATION

We dedicate this book to our Restless Genes DRD4-7R

"The compulsion to see what lies beyond that far ridge or that ocean—or this planet—is a defining part of human identity and success.

If an urge to explore rises in us innately, perhaps its foundation lies within our genome. In fact there is a mutation that pops up frequently in such discussions: a variant of a gene called DRD4, which helps control dopamine, a chemical brain messenger important in learning and reward. Researchers have repeatedly tied the variant, known as DRD4-7R and carried by roughly 20 percent of all humans, to curiosity and restlessness. Dozens of human studies have found that 7R makes people more likely to take risks; explore new places, ideas, foods, relationships, drugs, or sexual opportunities; and generally embrace movement, change, and adventure. Studies in animals simulating 7R's actions suggest it increases their taste for both movement and novelty. "

Nat Geo.com January 2013 issue

CONTENTS

	Acknowledgments	i
1	Out of San Francisco and into the Storm	1
1B	The Storm from Teri's point of view	Pg 26
2	Puerto Vallarta, Banderas Bay and Pecan Pie	Pg 56
3	"Sell a Pie, Go to Jail"	Pg 86
3B	Teri's point of view of Don's going to jail	Pg 116
4	Bucerias, Mexico	Pg 128
5	Freedom, Loss & the Power of Intention	Pg 154
6	Tonga, Australia, and Replenishing the Kitty in Sausalito	Pg 175
7	Trinidad and Carriacou on land	Pg 198
8	Carriacou on Water	Pg 224
9	Boquete and Bocas del Toro, Panama	Pg 253
10	Florianopolis, Brazil	Pg 279
11	Finding a home	Pg 300
12	Discovery	Pg 312

ACKNOWLEDGMENTS

Sheila G - for all those weekly meetings on the sailboat and for getting us started.

Jo Ellen M - for her memoir classes that helped us get started.

Kate W - for honest proofreading and encouraging feedback.

Carole D - for taking us to task with that red pencil and all the writing lessons crammed into the margins.

Howard B and Jim A - for proofreading from beginning to end with such dedication.

Sara W - for taking us under her journalist/novelist wing and supporting us to get it done.

Cole B - for formatting and tech work in between moving all those 2000 sheep around.

Chapter 1

Out of San Francisco and into the Storm

Whatever you can do or dream you can, begin it.

Boldness has genius, power and magic in it!

Goethe

My nagging fear had been replaced with a sense of calm. I hadn't noticed the moment of change but my turmoil about our little boat in this beautiful and horrendous play, began to soften. Around midnight, I had time to think about how and when the serious situation that we now found ourselves in began.

Teri and I met while sailing on San Francisco Bay on my classic wooden sailboat – a gaff-rigged, Friendship Sloop, *Galatea*. I was living aboard and working in Sausalito, where my business partner and I owned a small satellite TV business. The *Galatea* and I had been back in Sausalito for one year having spent the previous year sailing in Mexico.

Banderas Bay in Puerto Vallarta was my favorite place in Mexico. It was also *Galatea's* base. The 3000 mile round trip, between Sausalito and southern Mexico was *Galatea's* second trip. Although small, she was seaworthy with 150 years of proven design.

I was anxious to sail back to Mexico, but I needed to replenish the cruising kitty and help my ex-wife with our two teenage sons who were beginning to be a handful. I was glad I could help, but I still kept *Galatea* sailing on San Francisco Bay at every opportunity. A core group of local friends would gather at five pm and we'd all go out for a late afternoon sail, bringing the party with us.

It was on one of these night sails that Teri showed up, invited by a mutual friend and carrying two bottles of French wine. We became fast friends and started spending more and more time together. Several months later when I announced that I was getting ready to leave again for points south, she blurted out, "I want to go too."

Many thought that Teri, just divorced and with an enviable, established acupuncture practice in desirable Mill Valley, shouldn't drop everything and sail off to *wherever*, on a small, wooden sailboat with a man with a reputation... she had only known for a year! They cautioned that this was a very "Pie in the Sky" idea. Others thought it was brilliant and were ready to go themselves.

Politics in 1986, with its Reganesque trickle-down theories and the *Over Doneness*, of what was then the U.S., made us want to find something better. Compared with the simplicity and beauty offered by sailing and living on Mexico's Pacific Coast, it was an easy choice to make. But the biggest reason was that we wanted to cast our fates to the wind, looking for that *Perfect Place*. We wanted to rely on what we knew were our strengths – self confidence, creativity, and experience. We also wanted to see if we could make our way around the world, working as we went, as others had reported in Latitude 38, our favorite sailing magazine.

We took W.H. Murray's quote seriously.

"Until one is committed, there is hesitancy, the chance to draw back, always ineffectiveness.

Concerning all acts of initiative (and creation), there is one elementary truth the ignorance of which kills countless ideas and splendid plans:
that the moment one definitely commits oneself, the providence moves too.

A whole stream of events issues from the decision, raising in one's favor all manner of unforeseen incidents, meetings and material assistance, which no man could have dreamt would have come his way."

Having had several California –Mexico Sailing trips on different sailboats over the past decade, I had the experience to know the importance of timing. I wanted to sail the several hundred miles south into Mexican waters, in mid-November. This is an ideal time. However, serious improvements to the *Galatea's* standing rigging kept us in Herb Madden's Sausalito Marina for another three months.

We spent all the money we had put aside for the trip in preparing the boat and acquiring tools to be self sufficient. We loaded the boat with a tough and versatile hand cranked Phaff 130 Sewing Machine, lots of blue Sunbrella boat canvas, clear plastic window material, straps and snaps, grommets and hand tools. We had just finished making a canvas dodger for the *Galatea*, and felt we could do that and other canvas tasks, along our way.

Teri added a thousand needles from her now closed acupuncture practice. The available secure storage space for all this gear left little room for living. Our little 30-foot *Galatea's* waterline was soon lost beneath the surface.

Our preparations took us deep into winter, a bad time to venture into open waters. Nevertheless, we were intent to leave, regardless of the cautions. On a cold, clear morning in mid-February, 1987, we finally sailed under the Golden Gate and bid farewell to the Rat Race.

We were on a slow boat to warmer weather, clear inviting waters and the openness and smiles of the Mexican people.

Open Ended…

The weather was crisp and clear and the wind from the NW, pushing our little over-laden gaffer southward at a good speed.

We spent a day and night in Monterey acting like tourists. On our third day at sea, passing point Sur, the wind and seas began to build…

The skies remained bright blue with no clouds in sight. The increasing wind and wave height forced us to shorten sail (this reduces the area of the sail) so we secured the jib (meaning we took down the sail at the front of the boat) and ran with a staysail and reefed mainsail thereby using just two of our three sails). Reefing usually improves a boat's motion dramatically and so it was with the *Galatea*.

The motion of our over-laden boat was comfortable, but required my constant attention to the seas coming at the boat's stern from the north.

Because we didn't want water down in the cabin, Teri was down below with all but the top companionway board in place and the sliding hatch secured. She was essentially sealed in down below as a precaution in case we should take a wave over the stern.

I could talk to Teri and she could pass me snacks and things from the galley. She was reading Shirley McLaine's latest book and was content.

The boat was riding well, the big gaff mainsail, with one reef in, was boomed out full with a preventer rigged forward in case of an accidental jibe.

The small staysail was also out on her boom and blanketed by the main. As there had been no weather warnings about a storm from the Coast Guard, I was content to continue on with one reef.

As the day progressed, the wind and accompanying seas continued to rise and now in the early afternoon, I wished I had put another reef in when it was still possible. The situation and conditions now made taking another reef difficult as I couldn't leave the wheel to go forward to handle the sail and Teri lacked the heavy weather experience to be helpful and safe under these conditions.

The boat was flying!

The seas would barrel down on us from our stern quarter and each time the *Galatea* would raise her stern allowing them to pass beneath her.

The boat certainly showed her heritage that of a tried and tested fishing boat design from the northeastern US and used in the Atlantic fishing trade in the 1840s, long before motors.

Galatea was the first "Friendship Sloop" built on the West Coast. Nick Roth built her in a chicken barn in Marshall on Tomales Bay, just north of San Francisco. She was launched in 1964 and was built of mahogany on oak frames, bronze fastened and very strong and fast for her size, just over 30 feet on deck. I had sailed her to victory in class in San Francisco's Master Mariner's Race in 1984.

This was her third ocean trip down to

Mexico. The previous one – a 1500 mile return north to Sausalito, was done without a motor! Not easy against May's winds and seas.

All of my confidence in the boat's design and construction was further heightened due to the new rigging that held the sail and spars together. Although the work had made us late in leaving, it was a comfort to see how everything was behaving.

I couldn't rely on looking at the shore as we were out of sight now some 20 miles off the coast. That afternoon, most of my attention was on each oncoming wave, I wanted them hitting the boat on the stern quarter, not on the beam, or dead astern. I estimated the swells to be 30 feet, from trough to crest, with several feet of white water on the top of most of those waves.

I drank a lot of wine in those days and my son

Brad showed up a day before we left wishing us Bon Voyage. He had come carrying a box of red wine. Not your little supermarket box but an industrial/restaurant box! There wasn't room down below so we put it in the rear corner of the cockpit behind the wheel.

Up to now, I had been able to bend down between waves, turn the valve and let some red wine squirt into my cup. But this time as I raised the cup to my lips, a wave washed over my head and into the cup and filled the cockpit all at once. Luckily I was wearing my foulies and a harness tethered to a strong U-bolt in the cockpit. Thankfully, the last board in the companionway was already in place so no water got below. This sudden wave filled the cockpit before draining out through the self-draining scuppers and left me wet on the inside and out.

Teri would separate the top two boards a few

inches to talk. The sound of the wind and the seas was so loud we had to shout to be heard. Teri wanted some reassurance so I told her that all was well, I wasn't tired, and wasn't this exciting!

I didn't let her know that we were in a serious situation, one that I had no solution for except to hang on and, as they say in the Caribbean, "Sail de Boat, Mon". The seas were too big and close together for us to turn into them so we could reduce sail. So there we were stuck with what we had.

Teri wanted to know more about the storm. Her view from down below was all sky and water out the small portholes. She asked about the Coast Guard. I told her that she could talk with the Coast Guard – if she wanted to. Just to check in with them and give them our position. But I told her to say no more. "Let them know the boat is not in danger, and all is well". So Teri made contact and kept in touch with Monterey USCG throughout the night, and into the next day.

At some time during her conversation, the Coasties offered to send a boat to help us. I assured Teri that the last thing we needed, just then, was an over-eager coast guard cutter looming over us in an attempted rescue. One that I had hoped we'd never need.

We had too much sail up, and the last clear before-dark look at the mainsail revealed a sobering sight. Two reef points tied at the end of the boom had parted. As each wave passed beneath the boat, it would strike the end of our long boom, causing water to be splashed up into the sail. This looked like a bathtub's worth of water, trapped in the folds of the now unused portion of the sail. Every few minutes, the boom was jerked by the sea, sending a shudder up and down the rigging, the mast and my spine as well.

There was no easy solution to our problems.

The *Galatea* didn't have an autopilot, not that you could trust one to steer in these conditions anyway. We always steered by hand and stood real watches. I had been at the wheel since leaving Monterey that morning. It was now early evening and Teri was secured down below with Shirley's comforting prose. It was getting darker with no moon to light up this noisy scene. Also it was becoming increasingly difficult to keep the boat in the right attitude to the oncoming waves. Feeling the motion of the boat and anticipating the next wave became more automatic. But about every ten seconds or so, I braced for the possibility of a breaking wave to envelop me in the cockpit.

I saw that parts of the cardboard wine box were disintegrating and bits were threatening to clog the cockpit drains. So quickly I peeled the remaining box away from the real wine container leaving only a silver Mylar beach ball with spigot. Now, freed from its confinement, it was able to roll around the cockpit. Chasing and containing this ball with my boots and legs, finding the spigot, and trying to fill a cup between soakings and swallowing before lowering my head to prepare for the next soaking provided some comical relief. Did I mention that this was happening in mid-winter and very cold? Later, when we read about the storm, we saw pictures in the San Francisco paper showing the rail yards there at sea level, covered with snow. Freak weather.

Teri tried to feed me by passing a sandwich through the small opening in the companionway boards. She was still talking to the Coast Guard and they had asked her to keep calling on the hour. They informed her that this was a whopper of a storm and due to get much worse! The seas at harbor entrances were 22 feet and much larger 20 miles out where we were.

They again offered to send a cutter to our aid. She told them that the Captain had stated that no help was necessary but it was a comfort knowing that they had an idea of where we were. They gave us some numbers of wave height and wind velocities which were growing by the hour, and cautioned, in passing, that their cutter would take at least three hours to get to us. Not much solace!

Despite our efforts water was getting below decks. Teri reported it was sloshing over the floor boards. I told her to run the pump in short intervals to control the levels. Everything else seemed to be ok with her. She had the lee canvas up so she could wedge herself into our bunk, to keep from being thrown around. Occasionally a wave would be joined by another, coming at an angle to the usual direction and slap the side of the boat, knocking the *Galatea* over with the force. The boat always recovered and found her balance quickly.

If it weren't for the growing pain in my shoulders and neck from looking backwards and steering, it wouldn't have been too bad. As the night passed, pain, staying awake, and keeping salt water out of my wine kept me in a dream-like state. However, I did have time, to question my motives, qualifications and decisions that got us into this deadly serious situation we now found ourselves in.

We would never have left Monterey had we known of these serious weather conditions coming our way. But this particular weather pattern was not predicted by the Coast Guard as it came from out of nowhere. We heard four boats were lost in this storm. We were lucky!

The state of the noisy ocean around us was chilling. I have sailed all my adult life and I had never seen anything like it. On the top of the waves, all was blowing spindrift and white water. Our mast was well below the tops of these looming monster waves and when we were in the valley we estimated them to be well over 40 feet high. A survey, taken from my position in the cockpit, showed the boat was holding up pretty well, considering the conditions.

The loose reefs and bathtub full of water at the end of the boom was a big concern, but the renewed standing rigging held up to the jarring shake that accompanied each dip of the boom end into the froth of a wave top.

Wind velocity was now a constant 40 to 50 knots with higher gusts when riding on the top of one of these giants. Once the wave passed beneath us, *Galatea* would drop down at astonishing speed to the bottom between these bruisers, only to be borne up again on the next one and into the maximum winds again and the accompanying soaking. Froth and spindrift were blowing off the breaking tops and resembled a blizzard. The volume of noise was surprising and constant.

By ten o'clock the next morning, with the winds still increasing, I knew that we had to get the mainsail down completely, as the violent motion would surely break something soon.

I yelled for Teri to prepare herself to slither out of the companionway, which could be open only for the briefest moment, into the cockpit, and to take the wheel, so I could go forward and lower the sail. In order to do this, she would not only have to steer each wave perfectly but also needed to pull in on the mainsheet to pull the boom in so it landed on the deck, or cabin top at least, and not into the seas while I lowered the sail.

A gaff-rig is cumbersome with a long boom and a gaff boom that holds the top of the sail. In essence, two large flailing poles that could have easily knocked me into the ocean.

Teri performed her task admirably and although I gashed my hand, spraying blood all over the place, we did manage to lower the sail and secure it, with its boom and gaff on the cabin top. Greatly relieved, the speed and motion of the boat improved dramatically and for the first time in many hours, I felt things were, more or less, under control. Now we had time to deal with, what turned out to be, a rather superficial cut to my hand.

We were now running before the storm, with only our staysail. Our speed through the water was more manageable and our spirits lifted. At around noon, on the top of a very large wave, I thought I caught a glimpse of the top of cooling towers – could that be San Luis Obispo, and the reactor of their nuclear power plant, Diablo Canyon? What a relief! That says it all!

After a few minutes we rose again on a giant wave, this time, straining my salt-burned eyes, I looked carefully in that direction. The towers appeared again, abeam of us, to the east. Now it was a race to change course, without being rolled by what were now beam seas, and to try to make it to calmer waters. This we did with the help of our newly rebuilt little Albin diesel engine. After an afternoon of trying to clear the southern point, we finally made it into San Luis Bay and more protected conditions.

After what we had been through, it was

amazing that 12 foot seas and 30 knots of wind should feel like a millpond but it did! In fact, 12 foot seas never did seem large or threatening after that. We arranged to pick up a mooring and the Harbor Master came out and gave us a lift into shore. It turned out we were celebrities! He and his staff had been monitoring Teri's conversations with the Coasties all night and since another boat was also in trouble out in the storm, it made for exciting listening. One chuckle they got while listening is when Coastie talked to Teri and she said that "the Captain had spotted two cooling towers and assumed it was San Luis." He responded shyly and somewhat clumsily, "Did they look like a, ahhhhh, did they look like a lady's *brassiere*?"

Our boat was now safely at a mooring. The Harbor Master gave us a ride into town to a dry motel room, and a laundromat to wash and dry EVERYTHING from our soaking wet boat. Once we were dropped off at the town's motel, we entered our room and closed the door. There to see framed on the inside, instruction on what to do if certain alarms sounded! Instructions governing an accident at the very close Nuke Plant! Talk about "out of the frying pan and into the fire".

We were both exhausted after a 36 hour battle and were soon sleeping the sleep of the dead.

The next day was beautiful, the seas having calmed greatly, clear and cold with a good sailing breeze, and it was with clean and dry bedding and clothes that we struck out again. We rounded Point Conception and sailed into Santa Barbara to have lunch with Teri's Dad and stepmother Ruth. They were a bit dismayed but our enthusiasm could not be dampened even by such a storm.

We had many changes of weather on our trip

down the Baja peninsula, many stops at anchorages to enjoy, now that we had arrived in warmer waters. The days and nights were full of wonderful sights, catching fish, seeing many whales and the daily accompanying dolphins. The memory of the severity of what we had encountered faded as we sailed southward and the weather got a bit warmer.

We arrived in Cabo San Lucas at the southern tip of the Baja and had the birthday drinks I had promised at the Suicide Bar of the Finisterra Hotel. It had been a couple of years since my last visit and I was amazed at the changes that had taken place in that short a time, condos, new hotels, and a modern marina had sprouted up. It was a far cry from the sand streets and cobbled together shops, bars and restaurants of just a few years earlier. Nothing in Cabo was of interest to us and we were ready to cross over to the Mexican mainland and Puerto Vallarta, a two day sail in most weather, our journey was uneventful if you didn't count the tuna and Dorado caught along the way, or the hundreds of turtles we passed while they slept floating on the surface of a glassy sea, barnacles the size of tea cups adorning their shells. Approaching the mainland past the prison islands of the Tres Marias, we could see the entrance to Banderas Bay. We could also see a white Navy boat apparently waiting for us as it was barely moving. We didn't want to be stopped mainly because it was late in the afternoon and I wanted to anchor in daylight in the harbor still hours away.

Stopped and boarded we were: a double ender carrying several young heavily armed Mexican Navy sailors and their equally young ensign banged into the side of our boat as most scrambled aboard. We were still sailing toward our goal so Teri went down below to gather our papers. The sailors, not used to small, cramped quarters were anxious to search for drugs and return to their large and comfortable ship. One showed up with a shotgun shell which caused a sudden flurry of excitement until I produced the permit we bought at the Mexican Consulate in San Francisco just after buying a used shotgun at the San Francisco Gun Exchange before leaving. The sailors finally left and we were free to make haste for our first mainland anchorage of La Cruz de Huanacaxtle, 10 miles from Puerto Vallarta.

Chapter 1B
The Storm from Teri's View Point

"What would we do if a huge wave crashed over the whole boat?"

This is the question I asked Don the minute I saw his eyes blink open one morning in those January weeks before we left on our trip.

"What if the whole boat was knocked on its side?" I added.

I have a very vivid imagination and I had started to realize that we were heading out into an adventure of unimaginable proportions. Sure, we had been sailing the pants off the boat with all kinds of friends and colorful waterfront characters for the last year on San Francisco Bay – one of the more challenging bodies of water in the world… but now we were getting serious about sailing off "'round the world" or so we thought.

"It would bounce right back up like a little rubber ducky", Don would patiently answer. In fact he got used to my many morning questions as the hugeness of the undertaking set in with me. Morning and night, my mind was full of 'what ifs', wanting to know in advance what the solutions were so I could mentally file them away, relax and feel safe.

"You can rely on the proven design of the boat" he would explain still lying in bed on those cold winter mornings. Although she was only 30 feet on deck, she had ample head room for 6'1" Don and a wide, short cabin down below with a huge bunk that was soon to be my cocoon in the days ahead.

Since Don and I had known each other for just over a year, I was apprehensive about whether this adventure would turn out ok or whether I would be back in town in a short while trying to pick up the pieces of my abandoned acupuncture practice.

Of course, my father warned me against such an impetuous closing of my practice. I had done many things to create the practice I thought I had wanted. Then, after 11 years of practice, I was seeing patients six full days a week. It was exactly what I had worked so hard for and yet, a few years into this "success" I had found that I did not like being so bound in.

So many years earlier, right out of college, so many of my friends were traveling with

Arthur Frommer's book, *Europe on 10 dollars a day*, that I thought I could do it too. So back in 1970, I went to Europe by myself, flying Icelandic Airlines as we all did in those days. I had started in Amsterdam and worked my way solo down through Italy and Macedonia all the way to Greece before returning to England and then home.

So I had tasted freedom outside the US and knew how wonderful it could be to wake up on the beach of Ibiza with a nine cent shot of Terry Brandy or see the sunset from Mykonos, or visit the Impressionists in their museums in Paris. Now that I was in my late 30's, I was starting to reminisce about adventures I had had in my early twenties, just as my second marriage was starting to fall apart.

My soon-to-be ex-husband and I had decided to have a summer apart while he measured river flows in Montana for his Ph.D. and we were on our last bike ride together when we ran into a friend of his who invited me to join Don and his wild, friendly crew for a warm summer's night sail on San Francisco Bay.

Adventure with a capital 'A' was what I found that first night that I went sailing on the *Galatea*. I had a ball that night, drinking red wine and smoking a bit of marijuana with the gang and laughing and dodging freighters crossing back and forth across the shipping lanes that separated Sausalito from the gleaming lights of San Francisco's famous waterfront. It was all like a big, wonderful dream after living the previous few years on a Zen Practice Farm with its monastic lifestyle that included silent breakfasts and 4 am meditations. The change was so startling that I felt reborn with a sense of adventure I had not tasted since my travels to Europe 16 years earlier.

Don, an attractive blond with the kindest blue eyes and a distinguished manner was quite the ladies man in those days. Soon several different girlfriends would come and go but I just kept going out for sails on *The Galatea* as Don and I were "just friends" and it didn't matter to me who else came along. I loved the freedom of those night time sails, the wind in my hair, and the glimmering lights along the waterfront haunts I knew so well by land. The Marina area with the San Francisco Yacht Club, Ghirardelli Square and Fishermen's Wharf, Pier 39 and The Ferry Building all seemed to sail past us although we sailed past them with the Grateful Dead singing, "We may be going to hell in a hand basket, but at least we are enjoying the ride."

When my Zen husband returned from Montana after our summer apart, the breakup was inevitable. I moved out of the house in Mill Valley and shared a place with my dear friend Jennifer. We had met in acupuncture school 12 years earlier and still couldn't get enough of talking about acupuncture and healing patients and trying to figure out the whole world of Chinese Medicine. Again, a huge change of pace that was to portend of a deep shift in my life to come.

Free of my second marriage, I decided to take the plunge and asked Don if he would take me along when he sailed back to Mexico in the coming year. Closing my "successful" practice that was making me feel restricted, seemed to be just the right thing to do. We were, after all, just friends and seemed to laugh at the same things and to be able to finish each other's sentences. "Great minds think alike" we would find ourselves saying a lot.

After knowing each other for just over a year's time, we had flown down to Puerto

Vallarta and then driven down to Zihautenejo and back in a rented car for a couple of weeks to see how we traveled together.

We had a relaxed vacation and stayed in some very primitive motels on that road trip along Mexico's coast - there was little tourism there in the mid 80s. We explored and ate and drank our way along and ended up calling back home to extend our trip another week, we were having a much needed rest and it was so easy to be together.

I think that was the start of my opening up to a part of me that Don called *"B-a-d-d-e"*. Yes, having tried to be "Good" my whole life, this was a step into the unknown. It was liberating to 'just be'. Teri, the good girl, with the high achiever programming, was being given permission to buck the social conditioning of her upper middle class upbringing and go for broke.

And broke is what happened - because outfitting and repairing the boat for the sail down was what we spent most of our money on before we left.

We were glad that we got the brand-new 'Sat-Nav' navigation system and redid the standing rigging, which holds the mast in place using guide wires. It turned out to be our salvation to have the boat in such strong shape. But it meant that we left with very little cash because we could not face having to go back to work to make more money.

We felt we were talented enough to figure out something once we got to Mexico. After all, we had plenty of acupuncture needles and boat related sewing materials to use for our new 'sail repair business'. Little did we know how few dollars we were to make from what we thought of as our "two new money-making ideas".

When we arrived in Cabo San Lucas, I was anxious to try out my new acupuncture service to boaters. I used the Cruiser's Net to announce my services to the fleet. In most foreign ports where American cruisers tend to collect, the majority of the boat owners turn on their VHF radios at 8 a.m. every morning to greet each other and share information. Topics like: Who has just come in, who's leaving, questions about local facilities and where is the Immigration Office for checking in?

At the end of the 'cruiser's net', different cruisers will offer their services like outboard motor repair, etc. When I made an announcement in 1987 that I was an acupuncturist and happy to see people on my boat or theirs, there was the longest pause. No one ever came back on the radio to speak with me. I think that it was only about 10 years after the newsman James Reston had his experience in China with acupuncture and people were still unsure of this 'new' technique. In fact, the most common first question in those days was "Does it really work?"

Would I have just spent three years of training and eleven years in practice at something I didn't believe really worked? What a question!! But I would be very patient and kind in my response that 'yes, it really does work' and then the next questions were invariably, "does it hurt" and "why don't you bleed?"

Acupuncture is now so well accepted that I never hear these questions today. Hard to imagine we have come so far as to no longer call this beautiful, profound system of healing people for more than 5000 years, "experimental" or to wonder if it really works.

Don and I pay a lot of attention to "signs"

that seem to portend good luck and the Spirits watching over us. So as we sailed under the Golden Gate Bridge that clear, bracing February afternoon, we considered it a sign of good luck when the four fragile wine glasses, in unison, lifted out of their hanging holders by a very steep wave, all landed completely unscathed in the stainless steel sink three feet below. "Yes, you've done the right thing" we thought the Spirits were saying to us. "Freedom, here we come!"

There we were out beyond the Golden Gate Bridge and my imagined rough sailing conditions did not materialize on this, my first day of ocean sailing. Gentle swells like large meadows of water were moving us gently towards our goal of dropping the stress south of the border.

After we spent the night dockside in Monterey Bay, we headed out into an unsettled sea with sloppy waves and the sea sickness I had been dreading seemed to threaten and so I lay down to read the book my mother had sent me for the cruise, Shirley McLaine's latest book, *Dancing in the Light*.

As the waves started to build, Don seemed completely in his element and to be enjoying the ride. You could tell that he was glad to be heading back to warmer weather again after a couple of years in San Francisco. Dolphins were leaping and we were easing into boat routine even making sourdough bread as we went along.

We had talked of wanting to visit the northern coast of Brazil and the Healers of the Candomble religion but we were taking it one day at a time. Don had promised me a Special Birthday Drink at the "Suicide Bar" at the Finisterre Hotel in Cabo San Lucas. I had just turned the Big 4-0 in January and we had planned to celebrate my "mid-life crisis" with great gusto.

The waves started to build more and more and Don said that we needed to close the boat up so that we would not take seawater into the cabin below. This meant placing three boards, stacked one on the other to make a 'permanent' wooden barrier between us. Those boards being lowered into place were to mark the beginning of my 'being by myself' for the duration of the storm…the next 24 hours that would take us through the whole night and into the next evening.

We could communicate a little but the storm became so loud, as it built, that normal conversation was reduced to staccato telegrams like "do you want a peanut butter and jelly sandwich?" I would have to press my ear up to the tiny space I could make between the boards to hear his answer.

Having an ongoing conversation was out of the question.

The boat was at a 30 degree angle by now with the port side of the boat seeming to be "way down there" on the left. With the sloshing sound of the waves hitting the wooden hull right next to my bunk, I knew that we were moving extremely fast!

With no one to talk to or commiserate with, I put my full concentration into reading Shirley's book. The one passage I will always be grateful to her for was about the Eastern view of life and fate. She reminded me that when you look at life through the concept of Fate, that nothing can kill you if it is not your time to die and also, nothing can save you if it is! This can be oddly reassuring in such dire circumstances. There's a surrender that takes place and you can relax into it.

There we were in a washing machine of chaos

and breaking waves and yet it seemed to put my mind at ease to read such a simple concept. I never did feel terrified. In fact, Don was not upset by such severe weather pattern so why should I be? He acted like this was all very common. Could it be that this is how it would be for the whole trip to Mexico?? As time went by, the waves had built to unbelievable proportions and I tried to relax into the knowledge that the boat would perform like the little rubber ducky Don had predicted months before. It was probably a blessing that it was so hard to crawl up to see out the little portholes. With the boat at such an extreme angle, I could only glimpse the sea conditions for a moment at a time.

From my perspective the ocean waves looked like the water equivalent of the rolling downs of mustard fields outside of Stratford on Avon. They were rolling meadows made of dark green water and they seemed to tower at least five stories above our boat as we approached them from the bottom of the trough.

The waves moved towards us from behind, from the north, so I was not to see what Don was dealing with in the cockpit. Thank God for that! When we were at the top of these huge monster seas, there was so much space between us and the next cresting wave to the south that we could see vast distances down into the maw of the valley between the waves. It looked like our little wooden ship would go too fast to stop at the bottom but each wave would pick us up at the bottom and send us straight up into the steepness of the next wave. Unbeknownst to me, the waves at the top were breaking ON Don and the cockpit but I could not tell this from the cabin below and Don was so nonchalant in his conversations with me that I thought all was well and good, just very rough.

I tried not to look out too much at the sea conditions before it went dark. It was far more comforting to just lie back into my cocoon and read Shirley and her inspiring prose about Indian philosophy and her life changes. The way you can watch a movie on a flight and forget that you are on a vibrating airplane flying through space.

Don encouraged me to talk with the Coast Guard on our VHF radio and to apprise them of our location and the conditions. They could not have been friendlier and more comforting. They verified that we were just where 'Sattie' said we were. When this system, now known as GPS, was in its infancy, it relied on just a few satellites to give you your position on the globe.

Using this brand new satellite technology, we had to wait hours for the next satellite to come up over the horizon far enough to register our position. Satellites were often hours apart and you just didn't know for sure where you were until the next fix. The waiting could be tense.

As Don said, he encouraged me to stay in touch with the Coast Guard but made sure that I had been precise in my wording to them that "The Captain was not requesting assistance at this time".

These were the very words that I used when speaking with the Coasties each time that I would call them. They had encouraged me to request assistance as they said the storm was building and restated that it would take them at least three hours to get to our location, using their 95-foot cutter to come to our rescue. They asked me to stay in touch and call in every hour or so which I was grateful to do. It was very supportive to know that someone knew where we were and what was happening to us. Later the newspaper said that the two boats were lost in that storm. It dumped snow on the top of Mt. Tamalpais and shut down the Bay Area in the rarest of winter weather.

Don explained that there was little that the Coast Guard could do for us in the situation we were in. He said that he didn't want some young guys coming out and taking over our little wooden boat with its long bowsprit. One false move and the bowsprit, an eight foot pole sticking straight off the front of the boat, could be snapped right off in an instant and require days of repair in southern California.

In the late afternoon, the Coast Guard let us know that a huge commercial ship was nearby and would be willing to stand by if we wanted the help. They thought that the ship could create a protection from the wind for us but this didn't seem reasonable to us considering the severe conditions we were in.

We crested a wave and we both saw the ship way down in the trough of the waves. She looked like she was about one foot long because she was so far away and dwarfed by the towering wave above. We were lucky to be able to sail right behind her stern and not have her be a hazard to us. Had she been a little slower we might have had a difficult time not running into her side. As we got closer we could see she was over 600 feet long so we were dwarfed by her as we slid right by the back of her. Whew!

The most memorable event for me alone down in my little world below decks came as a big surprise to me. Because the boat was heeling over to her left side, as the angle became more pronounced I would take things down from the right side of the boat and wedge them down on the 'low side' to secure them. It went on for hours like this, the boat leaning severely to left, with books and things hunkered down on that 'low' side.

Then suddenly the boat seemed to be slammed by a big wallop and she bounced and then all hell broke loose and ALL that was down was now UP! The left side that I thought would be down forever was now way up in the air and all the things that were secured 'down there' were now falling on me and the 'new lower right side'. The most dramatic image was the box of wooden matches on the wall suddenly releasing all the matches at once from its cast iron holder, now freed they were all doing cartwheels in slow motion through the air, headed my way.

I was not hurt by any of this dramatic rearranging of our possessions in the cabin but this "being thrown on our beam end" was to teach me a very important lesson we would come to repeat many times over the next few years in Mexico "you never know what's going to happen next"!

Now, in our new position, the water that was on the floor seemed to disappear under the floor boards and I was able to wedge myself by squatting on the wet floor, so that I could slap together a fast peanut butter and jelly sandwich for Captain Don and send it out through the space made between the boards.

Somehow I was able to sleep fitfully through much of the night. I would awaken periodically with a start, wondering where I was and then call out to see if Don was still outside steering the boat or whether he had been knocked overboard and I was now alone in a raging sea. There was always that pause until he answered that took my breath away until I would hear him shout back over the waves that he was still there at the helm and doing fine. Thank God!

Don didn't seem the least bit concerned and so I wasn't feeling panicky in any way. I had been just hoping that this would come to an end sooner rather than later and that this would not be how the whole trip south would be. I was afraid to ask.

At day break, Don hollered for me to dress for the cold, put on my sea harness and come out to take the wheel so he could lower the sail and get the boat under control.

Like little Eva in the song, I crawled on my belly like a reptile and slithered my way across the cockpit floor and actually reached up from the floor to hold the wheel steady while Don moved to the side of the boat.

I prayed this part would be over soon so that

I could return to the safety of my bunk but there was another job I had to fulfill. As Don was lowering the sail, holding the wheel steady; I also had to reach out and pull in on the line that brought the boom into the boat so that the sail would not drop into the sea as he lowered it. This line was woven through a series of blocks that enabled me to handle such great force from my position on the cockpit floor. I never realized how much line was involved until I had to pull it all in under these wild conditions. All I was thinking about was how quickly I could go back down into the cabin and be out of the cold and wet that Don had just spent the last 24 hours in without respite or relief.

As I looked up at his pulling in the bathtub full of water that had gathered in our sail at the bottom, all I saw was a huge breaking wave coming for our cockpit and then a burst of bright red blood that seemed to cover the whole back of the boat with its unexpected scarlet brilliance. Don had somehow, in the chaos of it all, gotten his hand in between the boom he was lowering and another hard surface and caused a huge blood blister which then popped. What a show of RED. It gave me an immediate start to see such blood in a landscape of blue; luckily it turned out not to be serious and was easily managed after we got the sail down and the boat calmed in its motion.

As soon as Don took the wheel from me, I unhooked my lifeline from the hook and headed back down into the cabin, luckier than soaking wet Don who had to continue to steer us to each wave so that the boat was not swamped by the tops of the breaking waves.

He had many hours more to be at the helm that second day but at least it was daylight and we were no longer severely overpowered by our large sail. We worked hard at moving our boat into a tighter angle to the coast so we could hopefully make land fall at San Luis Obispo.

As it was going dark again for the second night we pulled into Avila. We were tired, soaked to the bone, all in the cabin was wet with sea water and of course we were very hungry. What an ordeal!

As we were headed to the motel, I asked Don the biggest question on my mind: "Is it always going to be like this?"

It was years later, overhearing Don telling the story of the storm at a party that I learned that this was the worst storm Don had ever been in in his 40 years of sailing!! Glad I didn't know that at the time!!

Had I seen what was really happening, I would probably have been quite alarmed.

Don's easy going manner was to set the tone for the whole voyage. In fact, for our whole life together over the next 27 years!

Chapter 2

Puerto Vallarta, Banderas Bay and Pecan Pie

We'd done it! After five weeks of exploring anchorages along the Pacific Coast of the Baja, we were finally anchored in La Cruz de Huanacaxtle, Nayarit, Mexico. La Cruz was a small fishing village just north of Puerto Vallarta on beautiful Banderas Bay. Only a 30 minute bus ride to Puerto Vallarta, La Cruz was really like being in old Mexico. We fell in love with this little village and its people.

We drank in the peacefulness of town from the cockpit of the *Galatea*. We loved the view from our at-anchor vantage among several other cruising sailboats. After a relaxing night we hauled anchor and set sail for Puerto Vallarta to check in with immigration and customs and to receive our cruising permit.

Banderas Bay, the largest natural bay in Mexico, is 400 square miles of water, bordered by a 60 mile horseshoe shaped shoreline along which lies the resort town of Puerto Vallarta and a scattering of small villages, some of which are accessible only by boat. At its Ocean side sits three large, uninhabited islands, the Tres Marietas. These islands, in addition to hosting countless nesting sea birds like the booby, act as a natural breakwater protecting the bay from the prevailing northwest seas. The bay is almost a mile deep and is a nursery for humpback and gray whales each year, along with an abundance of dolphins, tuna, dorado, jacks, wahoo and bill fish. It would be difficult to day sail on the bay and not spot constant marine life and the accompanying birds. Often you would see whales breaching, or slapping their enormous tails on the surface, in what most think is a form of communication. There is a constant presence of dolphins. In some spots of the bay, manta rays, with 14-foot wingspans performed flips in the air before smashing their black and white 2000-pound bodies down on the water's surface. Sometimes in early pre-dawn mornings, you could hear the splashes. Fishermen watch the diving birds to direct them to whatever was also feeding on the bait fish attracting them. The bay offered the finest sailing opportunity most sailors could wish for, fairly smooth waters and moderate and refreshing winds.

Sailing on Banderas Bay from La Cruz south

to Yelapa was always the perfect sail; great winds; protected from ocean seas by the islands, and waters so full of life, that it kept a grin on your face and the whole crew in a constant state of wonder and amazement. Dolphins, playing alongside, or swimming beneath the long bowsprit of the *Galatea* would accompany us as we skimmed along at hull speed. Someone on board would usually scramble to the bowsprit to talk with these magnificent creatures whenever they first appeared. Their antics, crisscrossing just in front of our bow, rolling on to their sides and giving us their curious look was always a delight. When sailing at night as we often did, the dolphins would leave sparkling trails of phosphorescence in their wakes, lighting up the waters around our boat. We always felt blessed by that contact, as if silently and privately communicating with some other worldly presence.

Out at the islands we'd anchor and swim with the manta rays. These magnificent graceful animals flash their startlingly black and white markings as they fly effortlessly through the waters. The rays liked to gather in one spot, in the lee of the largest island, and turn somersaults just below the surface. Once, Teri was able to free dive and touch one. This absolutely made her day!

Our dear friends, Joan and Bryden, lived in their 'Palapa in Yelapa'. They leased their land on the edge of a stream and built a magical home using all natural materials. Theirs was a one hour walk up the creek through the jungle. We'd spend a night with them, then haul anchor early in the morning and sail over to La Cruz and back, catching Dorado and tuna along the way. Fishing always accompanied a sail on the bay. It was usually fruitful, sometimes more than others, but always great fun. We had two heavy lines rigged for hand pulling at the stern deck with a variety of lures and three feet of surgical tubing to take up the shock of the initial strike.

Fresh sashimi was a staple at most of these sailing excursions. Once, with some former Navy Seals aboard, we hooked into a dorado that, try as we could, would not come closer than 20 feet off our stern. We could see it flashing the greens, blues and yellows for which the dorado is famous. He was a bull with a great flat forehead, and weighed at least 40 lbs. Two Rapala lures of different colors hung from his lower jaw along with our red and white $15 dollar Rapala still attached to our monofilament line, which in turn was wound from a now non-functioning reel, brought by one of the Seals. The dorado not only had broken free at least twice before with the lures still intact, but also had a large ugly scar on his dorsal fin where he had once pulled free from a gaff-hook. This was an experienced and wily fish.

We watched as he pulled and shook a great shake and broke our line! Frustrated, and beyond control, one of the Seals leapt, or rather flew, off the stern with a gaff hook outstretched in the direction of the fish, yelling, "No-o-o-o-o-o". No luck!

Over the years we lost many more fish than we were able to land but we shared many of our successes, usually cooked by a restaurant on the beach.

Living on our classic old gaffer at anchor just off La Cruz, we got to know most of the fishermen. They would leave early each morning as we were awakening in our cockpit and would return each afternoon with their catch.

We quickly assimilated. We were invited into

the homes and met the families of many of these men and became quite close with a few. We'd invite them and their families to come spend a day with us, sailing, drinking beer and wine; enjoying great music, a real vacation for these guys and their families.

As for Puerto Vallarta, we got to know the gossip, stories of ancient feuds, and how it was just before John Huston made the film, "Night of the Iguana." That film, and the presence of Liz and Dick and all the hangers on during its filming, is what first made Puerto Vallarta popular. Before that it was, like La Cruz, just a sleepy little fishing village.

We found small jobs but nothing of any consequence. We looked for boat delivery jobs. One showed up and we spent a few days sailing a boat from mainland Mexico over to La Paz on the Baja peninsula. During the trip, we talked a lot about our next move. We decided to look into starting a simple country style BBQ restaurant. We thought we might put it in the mango orchard belonging to the family of our new fisherman friend in La Cruz. We envisioned this in local style with a shady palapa-covered open space, with picnic tables, surrounded by blossoming or fruiting mango trees. It would be low-overhead, low key, serving great food in beautiful surroundings. We thought we'd have a good time doing it.

After arriving in La Paz and delivering the boat to her owners, we rented an inexpensive room and began to check out restaurants. We wanted to learn if this idea held merit. Teri had had some experience in catering – she worked with two English ladies who owned and ran a catering service for tour boats operating on London's Thames. She'd also had years of different levels of food business experience in California.

My restaurant experience was restricted to eating in many, and more recently, providing them with freshly caught salmon. My fishing partner and I fished commercially for five years out of Sausalito and sold all of our catch to the restaurants, direct for top dollar. You get to learn a lot about restaurants by seeing the kitchens in operation.

Teri and I both love food and its preparation. And we loved getting to know a favorite restaurant, and the people who made it memorable. There was an Italian restaurant just outside of La Paz that some fellow cruising sailors liked. They said it was owned and run by former sailing cruisers from California. We went right over and introduced ourselves. I have long forgotten that man's name but we are forever in his debt for the time he gave us that morning. It didn't take long for his horror stories of operating his business, from personnel not showing up for work to Mexican labor laws, to dampen our enthusiasm. Additionally, he reported that every gringo thought everything in Mexico should be one dollar. We quickly realized that opening up a restaurant was not what we should be doing when we returned to the mainland, and our boat in La Cruz. We were no closer to finding an answer to our income problems.

Gringos visibly working in Mexico were usually found in time share sales, something we disdained and wanted no part of. Others started their own businesses, travel agencies, property management, food export, operating their own shop, etc. These were areas that we had experience with, but no desire to get involved in.

One day, while walking the back streets of Puerto Vallarta we saw a banner hanging from the second story of an old building proclaiming, "Cooking with Jazz". We immediately entered a large, covered, open area that had been turned into a Cajun restaurant. We were told that until recent times this building had been a house of ill repute.

We ate a wonderful lunch and met Steve. He was one of the unlikely owners, a flamboyantly gay American ex-priest, now partnered with a Mexican ex-Federale. He told us his story of just opening this restaurant. Cajun and blackened red fish were very popular at the time in the U.S., but new to these parts.

They had been open for a year and had, they claimed, the best chef from New Orleans. The chef's excellent touch was evident in the succulent pork and sauces we tasted. Really wonderful! Later Steve revealed that the one thing they lacked was a great dessert. Teri piped up saying her mother's pecan pie recipe was a great one, and that if he was interested, we'd make one and bring it by. Maybe we could trade meals for it. Steve thought this a grand idea and welcomed us back.

During the next few days, we shopped for the ingredients, pie plates and a rolling pin. Pecans were available at some of the seed stores, but we found the pecans to be rancid, old, or not stored properly, totally unsuitable for our project.

We finally located a small seed store that promised to order some fresh pecans. A week later, we had our most important ingredient. Karo Syrup and brown sugar were also difficult to find. The Mexicans used piloncillo – a hard ball of dark unrefined sugar that would have to substitute for the brown sugar. It needed to be ground in our old hand-operated meat grinder. Karo finally appeared and at last we were good to go.

The pie crust recipe came from Julia Child. Now we were beginning to think that we might have found our niche here in Puerto Vallarta. We had been checking out other restaurants and their desserts, plus all the bakeries in town. There was definitely a need for great desserts here, as the Mexican products looked like they'd deliver, but all fell short of the mark. It seemed they all used the same bag of mix for everything they made. All were very disappointing, with a bad aftertaste.

We didn't have the room or proper oven on the *Galatea* so we decided to rent an apartment in the old part of town in a building owned by an Alaska salmon fisherman, Bob Brown, and his Mexican wife, Maria.

The rent took just about all we had left of our recent boat delivery pay, so we determined to give making American style desserts for Puerto Vallarta restaurants our full attention and our best shot. Our new apartment had two enclosed bedrooms. The rest was covered by a roof but open on the sides to the sounds, smells, noise and dust of the old part of Puerto Vallarta. The Mexican stove in our open air kitchen had an oven but no thermostat. The oven had to be opened frequently to make sure we didn't burn anything, not a good practice when baking. However, after many false starts, disappointments, and lots of rolled dough, we finally came up with a very fine product and our first recipe.

The night we showed up at the La Lousiane restaurant, with two beautiful pecan pies, Steve and his partner were hosting a grand opening of their new location, very "suave" and attended by many restaurant owners. We sat enjoying our dinner, but sneaking apprehensive looks at anyone being served a piece of our pie. These reactions amounted to love at first bite. These responses filled us with joy and excitement. People loved our pie. It became the talk of the evening. Some restaurant owners and managers came to our table asking if we could do desserts for them. We could hardly contain ourselves, assuring each owner that we could, even one who asked whether we could make a chocolate cheesecake for him.

The next few weeks were busier than we'd been for a long time. We were now turning out our signature pecan pie and scrambling to develop recipes to meet the demands of a few more restaurants. We were operating illegally. We only had tourist clearance on our boat papers; we had to leave Mexico every six months. We were prohibited from working or doing business without proper visas. We knew we were taking a risk, but we had neither the money to hire a lawyer, nor the risk of exposure to do the paperwork, so we just went for it.

Being totally out of money, we would rely on being paid in cash upon delivery, so we could go right out and buy more pie plates. We delivered the pies in a large clear Pyrex pie plate, so it was crucial to return with the old plate when the new pie was delivered. Ingredients, new molds for cheesecakes, etc. were taking all of the money we were making. We got to meet some of our neighbors and handed out samples of the latest creations, to judge results. Teri started giving acupuncture treatments to some ex-pats living nearby and used one of the apartment's bedrooms as a treatment room. It was a funny sight, Teri tiptoeing out of her treatment room to check whatever was in the oven baking, then assured, returning to her patient to remove the needles. It was her fine touch and experience that kept them returning and helped us pay the rent and purchase what we needed to continue to expand our line of desserts. We soon had several accounts, some of the best in Puerto Vallarta and word was spreading.

A typical day then would have us both preparing the day's orders, making only two at a time, our limit with the stove we had. Teri would have a patient to treat, and once the baking was completed I would pack the pies in Styrofoam boxes along with a blue ice block to keep them from melting in the steaming heat of summer. Carrying two boxes and six pies, I'd make our deliveries, get paid, retrieve our plates, and return to the acupuncture studio/bakery/home. After a glass or two of wine, I'd be off again to shop. Teri would join me if she wasn't with a client or working on a new recipe. Out we'd go to buy ingredients for the next batch. Our main shopping in town was everybody else's as well. At that time, Rizo's Market was the only market in Puerto Vallarta that offered more than soap and beans. Most of our ingredients were available there. We'd walk over to the dairy store and buy our premium butter in five kilo cartons, eggs in flats at the egg place, past the squeaking machinery of the tortilla shop and back home. Trips to the seed store were separate ones requiring a taxi and large bags of sugar and flour. We loved being out on these excursions, meeting new people, and seeing how things were done here. The heat of the summer took its toll, but there were always the pools.

The main beach hotels had large pool and bar areas, beautifully landscaped, maintained and staffed. Changing areas adjacent to the bathrooms were available to everyone using the facilities. As long as you looked like a tourist and were using the bar service, the hotels were happy to have you use the pool and lounge all day. We'd bus over and in 15 minutes be in the pool.

We were living from hand to mouth to be sure, but we were thrilled, certain we had really hit on something.

In between the baking, delivering, and shopping, I made time to make sales calls to numerous restaurants and some hotels. Typically, I would meet with the owner or manager and leave them with an entire fresh-baked creation, free to try on some of their clients. This was unheard of, but really well received. I would return the next day to see if we could do something for them; a very successful approach, even discounting my terrible Spanish. Sometimes the pies or cakes would go directly to a wife, girlfriend, or the mother of the restaurant owner we were trying to impress, but for the most part the approach worked. Soon we were figuring out what our next step would be. The oven we were using clearly wasn't going to help us grow. We needed a new place, a real oven, and proper refrigeration.

Like the Grateful Dead song, we needed a "Miracle Every Day". Teri and I were both strong believers in the power of intention. The presence of our need seemed to be enough to create our own miracle. Within a week or two Teri received word that property her grandfather had left for the kids, and almost forgotten about, had just sold. The property, two lots in the Florida Keys, had sold to a guy who wanted them only if he could pay cash! Teri's share in this gift would amount to a few thousand dollars!

We were tired of living in Puerto Vallarta with its noise and dust, and missed our boat. La Cruz, a half hour from downtown P.V., beckoned us to return. We aimed to have what we wanted, to live aboard at anchor in La Cruz, so that we could sail whenever we could find a spare moment. We would have to rent a place in La Cruz that would become our new bakery. We would have to buy a car to use for delivery and shopping. Would the joy of living where and how we preferred hamper our desire to grow our new business? That was our big question. Our last month in the P.V.apartment/bakery/acupuncture clinic would confirm our direction.

Work at the apartment in P.V. was now constant. It was summer and very hot. We slept outside, forced to scamper with our mattress into one of the airless bedrooms whenever the first large drops of what seconds later would become a tropical downpour hit our heads. As soon as the rain came, it would evaporate, leaving a very muggy environment. Occasionally we'd be awakened by a loud scratching noise that would turn out to be some unfortunate land crab trapped in our sink, attempting without success to claw its way free. Where did these creatures come from? Cats would prowl and howl from the rooftops. Every evening music would begin from one of the hillside restaurants, only to be out done by another band starting up along the same side of the hill, on and on, same songs, same sequence, now several different bands, different styles, all amped and bouncing off the hills and ridges around us. Very early, five a.m. or so, the gas station on the corner, up the hill, would empty a dumpster full of oil cans into the first garbage truck of the day. We longed to awaken in our quiet cockpit listening to the La Cruz fishermen passing quietly by.

Our business demanded that we hire and train someone so we could be released to create new recipes, experiment and sell. Adelina, the wife of an ex-pat, needed part-time work. She was a love and we began training her. From making the pie dough to prepping and cleaning, the addition of another enthusiastic pair of hands proved to be just what we needed. We soon added our second employee, Sherry.

Sherry had three children and an ex-husband. She had sailed down from California with the whole gang and now was adrift and in need. She and Adelina got along well, and the old girl of two weeks taught the new one what she had learned, and could jump right in learning by doing. That was our way.

The strain on the ovens was intense. We now had two going full-time. Sherry owned a VW bus that I rented from her so I could drive up to San Francisco. I wanted to find and buy a used commercial oven and bring it right back and put into immediate use. The restaurants were beginning to order more desserts as we increased our selections and we needed a big jump up in production. I found an oven in the used section of a restaurant supply place in San Francisco - a Blodgett convection oven capable of baking 16 pies at once! Oh joy! The oven was put on a skid and lifted by forklift, and with just a half inch on either side of the VW's sliding door opening, was gently placed down, all 700 pounds of it, on the floor of the van.

I wondered to myself while driving south how much money the customs guys at the border would demand from me to enter Mexico with my new treasure. Somehow a hundred dollars kept coming to mind.

Crossing the customs border station, I paid the agent $20 and he laughed in my face, and turned away; as he did I pulled four folded 20s out of my shirt pocket and handed it to him when he turned back to me. That was that, and soon we had real production going.

We moved the oven to La Cruz and our newly opened bakery there. Adelina and her husband and daughter already lived in La Cruz and Sherry and her brood rented a small house near the new bakery. We had found an unfinished house, no more than cinderblock walls with a slanted corrugated tin roof, dirt floors, and open barred windows. Forty dollars a month rented it from a woman who turned out to be the town's hooker. She agreed to pour a concrete floor; we hooked up electricity for the new oven and refrigeration, capable of holding all the cream, butter, cheeses, and finished cheesecakes that we had begun to make. Although life was becoming more complicated it was a joy to have an end of work at five p.m. and be free to experience the small village life of La Cruz de Huanacaxtle and to be reunited with our lovely *Galatea*.

In the morning we'd row our dinghy into the beach and tie it to a tree. Carrying our oars, we would walk uphill to our new bakery to start the day. On days we weren't cooking and delivering, we were experimenting or out selling. We received a chocolate cake recipe from a new older friend and artist, Katie Ottesen, who used to bake them for Carlos O'Brien's, a famous place in P.V. We approached them and got their business: three cakes a day! Now we were including cake and frosting in our selections, including pecan pie, three types of cheesecake; Kahlúa, Gran Marnier and chocolate, and now chocolate cake. We increased our delivery days to three and hired a third employee, a young married woman from the nearby town of Bucerias. Again Adelina's Spanish made training our newest employee feel right at home and made learning easier.

We were approaching the coming season, our first, and we felt we had a good selection of the very best American desserts we could make, seemingly unique in our part of Mexico. All handcrafted using the best ingredients available. We hired a local fellow to build tables for us and soon had a system of flow that worked perfectly. Prepping areas, mixing with three mixers, each capable of mixing ingredients for three pies at a time. These were expanded to five mixers so that we could mix up enough desserts to fill the ovens. Two or three people could handle that. Dough making areas and rolling by hand rounded it out. Cleanup was in a corner with a large sink and drain. We hired a dishwasher/cleaner from La Cruz. Chela had 12 children and needed time off from them, and some money to be able to feed them all. Through all of the commotion of settling in, and training new women, we sometimes had friends from Sausalito come down to visit and stay on with us. On those occasions we would pull out a large piece of foam and throw it on top of one of our work tables for them to sleep on. Our Mexican employees would be amazed by our funky approach to hosting visitors. We were bursting at the seams and in a short period we could see that we might outgrow this new place sooner than later.

It was time we got legal.

We were both wary of our exposure in town. I was a tall blond gringo who was seen entering all these restaurants with his arms full of desserts. That, plus the talk around town of our hiring people, made us increasingly uneasy. A Mexican woman friend recommended a woman lawyer from Mexico City to help us get legal. We formed a Mexican corporation and thought that we had applied for immigration status that would allow us to operate legally.

When we announced our plans to sail south from Sausalito some wags there said, "What a pie in the sky idea it was". When we had to come up with a name for our new corporation, "Pie in the Sky" seemed to be the perfect one.

Chapter 3

"Sell a Pie, Go to Jail"

Our first year of operating out of the La Cruz bakery was an exciting and joy - filled time. We loved meeting the townspeople, sharing our free samples, joining and being joined by fellow cruising sailors anchored off the town, some for the whole season.

We'd get to meet most of those sailors and their families and crew either as they found the bakery or at night sitting on the curb in front of our favorite taco place eating barbequed pork and chicken tacos for 10 cents each.

During the day we had a steady parade of people coming by, old, and young, mostly locals. We always had something for people to sample. For many of our local clients it was their first experience with American desserts especially these fine examples. Occasionally a Mexican or an American tourist would say they had sampled our desserts in P.V. and heard they were being made in the tiny village of La Cruz. They were thrilled to finally find us. Dr. Livingston, I presume! We never learned just how they did find us, as we didn't have any signs. We were operating illegally and worried that immigration would be alerted to our presence.

The first family we met in La Cruz was the Chavez family. One son, Jesus was a fisherman. He and a bunch of other local fisherman aboard a 50-foot fishing boat hailed us early one evening while we were having dinner in our cockpit. They asked us whether we had any diving equipment. We did. I swam over to them with my tank and regulator. They had wound a net around their prop and shaft; it was easy enough for me to cut it free. To them I was a hero; this simple act of neighborliness opened all doors to us in La Cruz. Jesus had ten brothers and sisters. Mama, in her sixties, held it all together with lots of help from her grown children. Most of the Chavez family lived with their husbands or wives right there in La Cruz. It was all very close.

Mama's youngest daughter, Betty, had some medical problem, and when she heard that Teri was an acupuncturist, she wanted to know if Teri could treat Betty. When we came for the first treatment, she hauled out two huge plastic bags of western medicines that had been prescribed to Betty over the past two years. They had tried everything. Teri treated Betty right at the family's kitchen table which stood on the hard-packed dirt floor.

Word went round that Betty was feeling better after her first treatment. When we returned for the second one, a crowd surrounded the entrance to the simple Chavez home.

We managed to make it inside to find Mama and Betty waiting for us at the kitchen table. The rest of the Chavez family, son-in-laws, daughters, and kids, crowded around, trying to get a glimpse of Teri's administering a needle to Betty's ear.

Treatment commenced beneath one dim, bare bulb, hung from a dark greasy rafter, beneath a corrugated tin roof, supported by a tree trunk sitting on the hard-packed dirt floor.

The home had neither a front nor back door. All eyes trained on Teri, and everyone talked at once. The neighbors who couldn't squeeze inside created a stir on the street. One grown daughter, Maria Luisa, asked Teri whether she could cure her husband's baldness. Her request unleashed a torrent of other requests, all in too-rapid Spanish accompanied by pointing to various body parts. She had to tell the disappointed daughter that there was nothing she could do for the spot of baldness on her husband's head, the better to nip those Miraculous Healer rumors in the bud.

We were invited to each and every household and for the many family fiestas held for so many reasons. Betty got well. Teri later treated Betty's two year-old niece for timidity with Bach Flower remedies.

Old man Chavez was a real character, an old timer bent with age but still, when not too drunk to move, very active. The family had, in addition to the little house in town, a grove full of older mango trees, about ten acres or so. It was across the road from the town at the base of the hill. They owned the side of the hill as well, and had sliced it up into long strips running from the grove at the bottom to the top of the 220-foot hill, which they distributed to members of the family. The view from the hilltop was spectacular, overlooking the eastern part of Banderas Bay, south toward Yelapa, and the mountains, and took in Puerto Vallarta.

One strip, perhaps a half acre, was for us if we wanted to buy it. The price was $7000. We told them we couldn't come up with that kind of money. They offered it to us for a cash down payment $1000, and whatever payments we could manage. Jesus' brother, Pedro, was in jail and wouldn't be released until someone could buy him out, bad luck for Pedro, but good for us and we went for it. At the time the real estate laws in Mexico were ambiguous, subject to interpretation, bribes, and politics. One thing, supposedly written in stone, stated a foreigner couldn't own land within 20 miles of the coastline. Another declared that *Ejido* land could not be sold. The *Ejido* is a farming group that occupies and works land but cannot sell it. This prohibition, long since ignored in La Cruz, was still the law. Our informal handshake contract with the Chavez family ignored these laws and was one we all drafted sitting around the kitchen table. Not your accepted real estate practice for sure, and although we had reservations about the old man's ethics, we placed our faith in Mama's honesty.

We didn't have a plan for the property, how or where to build on it. There were many challenges due to the steepness of the land but we enjoyed scampering up, sitting, gazing, and drinking red wine there. While sitting there on the land, we would find artifacts. Many shards, some with designs or parts of designs, some pieces still with paint, we'd pick out of the earth with our fingers. Blues, ochre, and reds were the predominant colors. Most exciting were the many translucent dark gray obsidian blades. These small, rectangular blades were beautifully crafted with a flat, beveled but still sharp edge. Some were three inches long and in perfect condition. We heard that these artifacts were hidden when that hillside had been used to grow pot. The frequent summer rains would wash away some of the soil and leave these treasures exposed.

Although we were never to build on it, just owning this land would save us years later, in another land.

Our second fisherman friend, Martin, always seemed more serious and adult to us than his mates. We'd met while rowing our dink in to the beach each morning to begin our work day at our new bakery. We'd pass his corner house and stop to practice our horrible Spanish with Martin and his family.

Martin was older than most of the fisherman in La Cruz, over 40, tall and thin, a widower, with two children. He lived in the old family casita with his aging mother, across the road from our new friend, Jesus. Although growing up together, they couldn't be outwardly friendly with each other due to an ancient family feud involving a murder, although we didn't realize it until years later.

Martin was among the crew of one *panga* (the local open workboat) that left La Cruz with three other fisherman plus 1000 pounds of ice carried amidships in large, worn plywood boxes. These boxes were covered with worn shreds of canvas protecting the ice from the tropical sun. The open boat and crew would be accompanied by at least one other boat, sometimes two, for safety. They would run from the La Cruz fisherman's co-op to the "forbidden" Islas Marias some 50 miles away. They would stay out for as many days and nights as was necessary to fill their boxes with three tons of iced snapper. Then the challenge was to run back to the safety of La Cruz without sinking in their overloaded boat.

A trip to Islas Marias was risky business. This rich fishing ground was off limits. One of the Maria Islands was being used as a prison. The surrounding waters were patrolled by the Navy.

Out there 30 miles from home base, they could not legally land on these little islands. If serious weather threatened, they would risk having their boats, prized motors and their hard earned catch confiscated and jail sentences on top of that. Such was the difficult life of the La Cruz fishermen, trying to supply the local restaurants with the popular red snapper that tourists clambered for. If the visitors had only known what great risk lay behind their "bargain" red snapper dinners!

All this very hard work and tremendous risk was taking its toll on Martin, he told us one day. It started us thinking.

We liked Martin and his family, and Martin liked Sherry, our first American employee. Sherry, mother of three, was a very attractive blonde. Having separated from her husband, after their family's adventuresome sail down from Santa Barbara, Sherry had no idea how to support herself and her three kids. She was in need of attention, training, money, and as it turned out, Martin.

It all seemed predestined for us to offer Martin a new direction, less taxing and closer to his new girlfriend. We offered him a job at our small but growing, "Pie in the Sky" hidden bakery. He became our go-to guy, that of deliveryman/salesman/shopper. Once trained, it would release me for other pressing needs. It all came together nicely. Martin proved to be a quick and eager learner. He helped me with my terrible Spanish, grasped our intentions, and the bigger picture. Having such a real Mexican character as my new sidekick helped me to be more accepted. Whenever the "gringo" bakery guy came by with Martin there were lots of jokes, laughter and drinking over lunch in Puerto Vallarta with other fishermen and ex-fishermen, some of whom were now running the new restaurants that were popping up in town. Many of these guys knew Martin as a fisherman, and would tease him about his new job.

It was hard, sweaty work, delivering to our clients, taking orders, making at least one sales call, with one of our creations left behind as a calling card. The shopping required stopping at three or four locations, a drive of some 40 miles round trip three days a week. The temperatures and humidity would take their toll on the delivery guy walking in the blazing sun lugging desserts from wherever we could park, to the restaurant itself. Although the Mexican men were oblivious to the extreme heat, my shirt was always stuck to my skin when I went out with Martin.

The pies, cheesecakes, delicate tarts, and other items were packed in white Styrofoam boxes to protect them from the rigors of delivery and the heat of the day. We used frozen blue ice packs on the bottom to hold the temperature down. The delivery car would be packed according to the route. Accessibility was of prime importance. We supplied most of the most popular and better restaurants by this time and were calling on some of the larger hotels.

It was a treat for us to see and better understand the local culture, as we watched our few Mexican employees pull together, laughing and joking, while helping the delivery guy pack up each morning. As we expanded, adding more local women employees, mornings in the bakery would sound like chatter from "the bird trees" we passed under on our early morning walks. Some trees would hold hundreds of birds, and at certain times in the early morning, would resound loudly with chatter and fluttering.

Once packed and on the road, Martin and I would talk of local history, of fishing, and of the many characters he knew. We did this with little common language but much understanding. We also planned the day as well as we could, hoping for as few surprises as possible. There were always surprises; the biggest one was on the Friday that I was arrested!

When Teri and I could see that this idea of an American dessert bakery was a good one, we decided to get legal as soon as possible. Operating as we were, with only tourist visas was a huge risk. We'd been deluding ourselves thinking that we were invisible when the opposite was true. We needed the protection of a Mexican corporation and working visas for the two of us if we were to be serious about growing this business.

A Mexican friend recommended a woman lawyer from Mexico City to us and we got together with her to begin the process of legalization. Now with a bank balance from the sale of grandpa's lots, we paid $3000 upfront for the whole immigration package. It was to be a two-part process. The first part was easy and that was to create a corporation. This creates a legal Mexican citizen with rights. This Susana did for us and it went smoothly. The second part, where the corporation requests our management services to run the corporation, should have lead to our working papers. Unfortunately, part two was never realized. Unbeknown to us, our lawyer had gotten herself into trouble as part of a legal group that tried to take on a local honcho. Too bad for us! We now had legal invoices which the restaurants required. However, we were still left in the category of working without papers. Still in jeopardy, we continued to work until we could come up with more money and another lawyer.

The Friday I was arrested by Immigration

Services, I was walking into the rear entrance of the oldest and most famous Puerto Vallarta seafront restaurant, Las Palomas. Martin and I were caught red-handed, both carrying Styrofoam boxes filled with cheesecakes. The immigration officer flashed his badge as he approached me and said that he was arresting me for working in Mexico without papers. That made my heart skip a beat! As I stared dumbly at the guy, trying to catch my breath, Martin attempted to defuse the situation, first with humor and then taunts but to no avail. Some of the kitchen staff from the restaurant, drawn by the excitement, began to pour out of the back door and onto the street. Everyone had an opinion and voiced it at once. At one point the immigration guy asked Martin why he was standing up for this gringo. I told Martin to continue without me and to finish up and go back to the bakery. With the sounds of jeering and some laughter behind us, Officer X and I walked across the street into the Office of Immigration.

It is a sign of just how naïve and complacent we had become after three years of living in Mexico, to be delivering right across the street from the Immigration office! Once inside, I asked if I could make a call before being led off to jail, and that being provided, spoke briefly to Teri. Telling her what had happened, I asked her to gather all the legal papers and come down to Immigration and to tell the truth.

The Immigration Officer was aggressive when driving me to jail, questioning me about dates of my entries and departures into and out of Mexico; about the bakery, our clients and the like. I asked him if I was going to jail and after he said "yes", I told him I just couldn't remember a thing.

The jail was an unmarked, drab three-story

building situated in an unfamiliar part of town. Once inside and processed, I was taken upstairs to the top floor. Not knowing what awaited me, I saw a beautiful blonde woman sitting alone inside one of the cells I was passing. I looked her full in the face as I passed and I saw the fear in her eyes. All of this added to the uncertainty of the situation and then we arrived at the end of the hall. There was a worn, steel door with bars on the top half and it was inside for me!

The room was a rectangle 60' x 30' with concrete bunks, lowers and uppers, built into the wall. There were around 30 men crammed inside, all of them Mexican and young. At 50, I might have been the oldest person there. Summoning all my Spanish and taking a 50 peso note out of my pocket, I took a few steps toward the center of the room, and plopped the note down on the floor for all to see, while stating it was for all to use as only they would know how.

Looking around, I asked no one in particular where I might sit. Someone motioned to the end of the room where four bunks were built into the wall. Two uppers - two lowers, I took an empty lower. Once I sat down on the slab of concrete that was to be my lower bunk for the night, I took a look around the room to see barred openings under the roof to the top of the walls allowing air to circulate. Not much circulation in June. The conversations, halted upon the arrival of the new gringo, resumed, and after a short while, grew in volume, intensity, and animation. Young street hoods, petty thieves, selling drugs, mainly pot, accounted for most of the population in this cell. There was much bragging, much machismo, being flaunted around this group. Many knew each other and the sound of confidence grew as well as the volume, broken only when the guard came for someone or just to look in on the cellmates. All were very curious about me. Gringos are seldom arrested and once they heard that I was brought in by Immigration, they all cracked up laughing. Poetic justice, a gringo wetback!

Things relaxed and I started to feel accepted by my outlaw brothers. I settled in and wondered what Teri was up to. I knew she'd be upset, but doing all she could to get me released. I knew that I was about to be deported but since we had formed the corporation I hoped we could work out whatever was necessary to continue the outlaw bakery.

Later in the afternoon, a guard arrived with a bundle for me! It contained a pillow and a blanket; a bag with a toothbrush and toothpaste. The guard told me that it had just been dropped off. In Mexico NOTHING is provided to prisoners. Someone must bring all these things to you at the jail.

Teri had included a couple of pieces of fruit and a candy bar. I was grateful that I could now lean on something soft but the last thing I was, was hungry. So I laid out the fruit and candy and told my cellmates to help themselves. The food was scooped up immediately but a moment later one fellow inmate slid up to my bunk and handed me a candy bar saying that it was for me. I'm not interested. I tell him to share it. "No, No, amigo, it is for you! – And just when I'm about to decline more forcefully, he stated in a whisper that there is more there --"a note"! "Thank you, Amigo". I sat back down and to my surprise Teri had sent me a note. "I am not worrying" it began – well, that certainly is a strange beginning, I thought. Great for her but she's not in jail!! It went on to say that she was with José Luis and they were working on getting me out of jail. At least that was what I thought it said. I didn't have my glasses with me so I was not completely sure and there was no one to ask to read it to me. Teri said that she was working with Sherry and Yasmin to finish the baking for Sunday's sail. In all the excitement of the day, I'd forgotten about our first big catering job for a party hosted by a bigwig local hotel owner on an antique sailing ketch out on Banderas Bay for the World Cup game. This being late Friday, we had only one full day to finish preparing for that event along with our normal Saturday baking pattern. Shit! What a time for this to happen.

The summer is a very slow and difficult time for the Mexican beach resorts and it was hard enough just to survive, without problems like this. I realized it would be dark in a few more hours. It dawned on me that I'd be spending the night and I was beginning to feel a little hungry when the guard came around with more gifts for the gringo. Takeout cartons from a place unknown to me, but was attested to by my immediate neighbors as being one of the best. I was honored and glad to have something substantial to eat and grateful to my wonderful wife and friends who made it possible. Shortly after I'd eaten, boredom overcame the youngsters and many suddenly showed up at the foot of my bunk with several having quickly climbed up to the top bunk over my head. It happened so fast that I didn't have time to be afraid as the attraction turned out to be not me but the poor woman in the next cell.

To be able to see through the three-foot high barred opening at the top of the wall, the boys had to climb my bunk to look in at Mariposa.

Solo and naked, there dwelt a mad woman. My young toughs began taunting her with phrases, undecipherable to me, until they got the response they came for – upsetting Mariposa enough to do or say something outrageous.

From my cave below all the action, I didn't know what the last straw was for Mariposa but she caused much laughing, screaming and a quick retreat from the top bunk, with boys falling back to the floor of our cell. This first group of taunters went, followed by more who had missed out on the first episode. Like the first act, the scene repeated for all except me – and possibly Mariposa!

After a few more attempts the taunters retreated back to their bunks to find other amusements before dark.

All had appeared to return to normal when suddenly I saw water dribbling down from the bunk above. Slowly it increased to a thin sheet of water, veil like, it poured past me on my bunk. I realized that I was INSIDE a small thin sheet of water, falling past my bunk. How was this possible? Then it struck me: this was PISS, not water!

Mariposa had struck back at those who would disrupt her serenity, by throwing her pee pot up at those faces through the bars; it then landed on the top bunk, and held me prisoner in my bunk until it stopped. Fortunately it only fell onto the floor and not onto the lower bunk or my blanket.

A well-meaning cell mate showed up with a mop from the one commode toilet, open to all, at the other end of our long, bleak cell. The mop was more disgusting than the pool of piss, and when all was swabbed together, it created an odor I was forced to get used to that night. Piss happens!

On Saturday, I was summoned to the office downstairs. I'd seen some of my cellmates return very bruised from visits downstairs and I was not my usual calm self approaching the Commandant's office. The situation was beginning to make me wary, on this, my second day of incarceration in a Mexican jail.

Rounding the corner, much to my surprise, there was a friendly face! Oh joy! It was Kathy Von Rohr and her son, Kiki. She greeted me outside the Commandant's office, telling me that he was a friend and that we could talk freely right there. "Now you're a true Vallartan", she told me, and "one who has spent time in the old, beat up Puerto Vallartan jail." Kathy told me that she had heard from Teri, and that Jose Luis and his brother knew my tormentor, the Immigration guy; they had arranged my freedom with a thousand dollar bribe. Trouble was I knew we didn't have a thousand dollars. Kathy said that Kiki was going up to the States, but that he could postpone his flight a day or two and that I could use his dollars to come up with the required thousand U.S. cash. That was all she said. (In the days before ATMs and with all the banks closed on the weekend this was a major miracle.) She had to leave quickly, saying over her shoulder, that everyone had heard and wished me good luck! I still didn't know my fate, only what she had told me.

I returned upstairs with a grin, not a bloody nose. Later that afternoon, all was revealed to me as I was released into the open arms of my sweetie, and received big abrazzos from Jose Luis and brother Alfredo - our friends who made it all happen.

We returned to their Islas Marias restaurant with its soaring conical thatched palapa roof, directly across from the Puerto Vallarta Airport. We had started with rounds of tequilas when I was told how my freedom came about.

We will always be indebted to those two who, knowing how things are done, had made the right calls to get it done. Nothing feels as good as freedom! We had little time to celebrate however, because we were way behind in our preparations for the next day's gig.

We finished in time and before long we found ourselves standing on the teak decks of the very varnished, "Kathy Marie", a magnificent 80 foot ketch, once a gift from the British Government to the Princess of Siam. Gold-plated dolphin faucets in the heads, oriental carpets throughout, with much shiny brass, all contributed to the elegant ambiance. A first class outing it was, with the very best from "Pie in the Sky."

Teri and I stood on the port side deck as we

cleared the breakwater on a boat filled with some of the more powerful hotel owners in Puerto Vallarta.

On our way across the bay to Yelapa, we were looking up the hillside streets, still wet and shiny from a passing shower, looking for the building that was the jail. Once located, we raised our champagne glasses in a toast to my fellow cellmates, and to Mariposa, up that hill, in that building, right up there.

Chapter 3B

Teri's Point of View of Don's going to Jail

When the phone rang, my hands were covered in caviar. Rolling little balls of cream cheese into caviar transported me back to my catering days on the Thames and yet the insistence of the ringing phone brought me starkly back into sweltering hot Mexico, two days before the 1990 World Cup match would begin in Italy.

We had our first request to cater a party for several of the owners of the bigger hotels.

The party was to take place on the deck of an elegant yacht, hosted by another big mucky muck. Our friend, Lee Gibson at Los Pericos invited us to put on the dog while these powerful, Latin men watched the World Cup, lived it up on champagne and caviar balls and cruised the bay along its quaint waterfront towards Mismaloya. The opportunity to expose this group to our American way of doing food in those days held great promise.

I was shocked to hear Don saying at the other end of the line, "I've just been busted and I want you to get the papers of the corporation, passports, all that you have, and come down here and tell the truth." That was all he said before he had to go.

Stepping back into caviar world, I felt unreal. Right in the middle of the chaos for this party, I had to think about Don's having been busted by the police. Wow!

Our whole bakery was thrown off schedule with this party planning. We were making recipes that Yasmin had not made before. How could I leave her with my American friend Joan who spoke hardly a word of Spanish and step into the world of not having working papers in a place we've been living in and working in, "illegally", for three years?

Having no filing system in those days, the Mexican way, just in a stack of file folders, it took awhile for my trembling hands to find the ones I needed. I hardly remember the 20-minute drive into town. My mind wandered all over the truth of what to say, how to explain that our disappeared lawyer years ago did only the first part of getting us legal. Yes, we did, thank the Lord, have a corporation of our own with the three required Mexican partners. However, we didn't have the proper immigration clearance to be working it. So now we had to face the music. We had joked about it many times, what we would say if we ever got busted. Now the joke was on us.

I drove straight to Immigration on that sweltering June day with the sun beating on me, the breeze blocked by the ocean front restaurants and apartments. We had never been into the Immigration office because in those days, a powerful woman sat at the front desk and ruled the roost. We had heard that a Mexican government official sat in the inner office. This person was changed regularly by Mexico City 'to avoid corruption'. But the real power in the place belonged to front lady, Alicia. She never changed. She had the manner of a drill sergeant. Her frown mixed with disdain was more withering than the heat. Alicia had been pointed out to us once across the square. There were no forms that you could get to fill out and apply for immigration status that would allow you to work legally. Once you were in there, you were a marked person, according to the rumors and horror stories bandied about in the gringo community. If you asked to apply to work, Alicia started with a slowly written list of documents you could never reasonably gather. Then once you had been in, well, if you didn't get the permission, then what? We gave Immigration a wide berth. We were lulled into passivity by the three years that we had gotten away with it.

We thought that living way out of town, twenty minutes beyond the airport, way up over the state line in Bucerias, that we were invisible to Alicia. Only later did we learn that she not only lived in our town of Bucerias herself but that her grandkids often bought our bakery treats as did she. We were living in La-La Land.

So here I was, headed to Immigration for the first time ever, and the door was closed and shuttered. There was no sign on the outside of this building to let you know it was a government office, much less with posted hours or who to phone in case of an emergency. Realizing on this desolate Friday noon time that no one would be back here until Monday morning, the street defeated me with all its heat and dust, and its closed Mexican walls/doors. Not a soul to be seen. I wept.

Someone came along and told me to check in the basement parking lot of city center just down the street, a few blocks. Strange as it sounded, and dark and foreboding as it was, I managed to pass all the drunks and rowdies hanging just outside the entrance to the police station. All stopped as I entered because everyone wanted to hear what the white gringa was going to say. All the police behind the counter turned to hear me say in my mediocre Spanish that I was looking for my husband who was taken to jail by immigration. They froze for a minute and then someone started to check the roster and another went to ask. A tall, gringo with a mop of white blond hair stands out at 6'1" amongst black-haired men who stand a Mayan half-foot shorter than Don.

No, was the answer. They did not have him there; they didn't know what I should do. I didn't cry again until I reached the dank car park area outside the jail but it was with tears in my eyes that I headed north to see our compadre, Jose Luis. He owned the rib restaurant at the extreme north end of Puerto Vallarta. He was a good friend and a wonderful family man and made the best ribs in town.

Luckily for all of us, Jose Luis and his wife Mari spoke very good English. I blurted out my sad tale, desperate to talk to him. I couldn't find him and had no idea what to do.

Jose Luis went right into action. He called to Xavier, the young bartender, to bring me a nice big shot of tequila and a lime and chaser. In the quick transition from caviar to the ominous jail under the civic center and all the driving around, I had not eaten that morning. The tequila was to calm my nerves, he explained and I was not to worry. "Do-ant worry" he would say and follow up with it in Spanish, *"no te preocupe"*. Don't worry, Teri, and off he went to consult with his brother, Alfredo.

A good strong shot of tequila will settle you down in a hurry, especially on an empty stomach. So I was starting to relax when Jose Luis returned to tell me that Alfredo did know the officer who arrested Don and took him to jail. He knew where he was being held and we would go there right away, "just wait".

He snapped his fingers and the little Mayan bartender came over and served me another big shot of tequila. Don't worry he said and the Mayan smiled and the words seemed to reverberate in my head, floating on top of two good shots of a great local drink, known for its potency.

Just as we were about to leave in his car, Alfredo came roaring into the back lot and they huddled and went into the office. I could see Jose Luis snap his fingers to the smiling Mayan who looked like he came to serve me directly off the glyphs of Palenque. Don't worry he said to me and tequila appeared in its cobalt blue rimmed shot glass. The tall conical roof of woven palm leaves grew taller as I waited for the brothers to return. Return they did and off we all went. Jose Luis and I were driving into town and Alfredo went off to meet with the officer and make the deal.

I was, of course, worried about the jailers beating up Don. Oh, no, Jose Luis assured me that they wouldn't do that. "Don't worry, Teri, don't worry." We can work this out.

All of this information seemed to float toward me as we bumped our way down the uneven cobblestone streets, into the hotel zone and then up a street off the main thoroughfare.

When we pulled up in front of another unmarked three-story building, I had no idea that we were where Don was. Jose Luis suggested I go into the little corner store and buy some fruit and a candy bar so I can write a note to Don. I was mystified.

I stumbled down into this store, drunk as a skunk, slurring my words, I asked for a *barra de chocolate* and picked up a couple of oranges as I was instructed to do. I didn't know what to say to Don except the phrases that were repeating in my brain, and I started the note, in my haze with "Don, I'm not worrying". With three tequilas in me on an empty stomach, all I could do was repeat the phrase I had so often heard all morning long. What a thing for him to read.

Then, when Jose Luis came back, he explained that we needed to go to the good seafood place on the corner and get Don some food. He would be given no food inside the jail. We got the big take out cartons and delivered them only to learn that now I had to go home to Bucerias. I needed to gather up some blankets that I would not want back and a disposable pillow otherwise Don would be sleeping on hard concrete with only his hand for a pillow.

Streaking out to the bakery in Bucerias and back, just time to gather bedding and head back, I commented on what my friend Joan and Yasmin were making for the party. They were on their own, Don was my first priority. I hardly slept that night. In the morning, I hastily installed my two friends in the kitchen. We still had this one day to complete the cooking for the party. Don was released in the late afternoon. We went straight back to Jose Luis's restaurant and laughed and told the story from every angle and all the pieces made us laugh over ribs and more tequilas.

The next day we were hanging with the other extreme of the hierarchy of Puerto Vallarta. We were to be deported in a few days, but for today we were on an elegant yacht, sailing on the bay, drinking champagne and eating caviar and we didn't care what happened next. Robert Frost when asked," What were the most important things in life", was quoted as saying that the first most important thing was "to be out of jail". We agreed.

CHAPTER 4

Bucerias, Mexico

The reason we were in Bucerias before we were busted was because Janet, Phil's widow, the American partner of "Dos Felipes" showed up saying she wanted to rent out the other side of her duplex in Bucerias. She offered to rent her guesthouse to us to use as a bakery and a home. It was located only five minutes away from La Cruz, we jumped at it.

Bucerias, also on the shores of the Bay, was much larger than La Cruz and it was on the only coastal highway of Mexico. Highway 1 was only two lanes at this point- with Puerto Vallarta an easy 30 minutes to the south. Bucerias featured a Catholic church, a town square and a beachfront with several restaurants. It was big enough to support a taxi stand and a video rental store. We always thought of it as a quiet, uninteresting village and never spent much time there.

We did, however, stop to buy the barbecued chickens from the chicken ladies of Bucerias. Several of these women had set up barbecues right on the highway where they offered cooked chickens with lots of fresh tortillas for just five bucks. The cloud of chicken cooking smells, along with the mesquite charcoal smoke from several open fires would always draw the passing traveler. Being a favorite of the locals, and something they could afford occasionally, it was a popular gathering spot.

We liked them even though they were referred to by some cruisers as Dusty Chickens due to the thin coating of road dust some received while cooking.

When we were considering whether this change could work for us, we came to see more of the town, off the road, and came to appreciate all it had to offer. It was closer to Puerto Vallata and our clients. It also had a larger labor pool and yet was still close to the peace and quiet of our boat at anchor in La Cruz.

Bucerias also had a magnificent white beach, level its entire length of shore line, which was the best for morning and evening walks.

A friend had a trailer he was bringing down from San Francisco and asked whether we needed anything that could be brought down on it. We decided to find another used

Blodgett commercial oven and have him bring that down. The day it arrived, we went to the La Cruz baseball field and waited for the game to end and invited the local ballplayers/fisherman to the bakery for beer and sandwiches.

All we asked was a little help moving our 700 pound oven! We held our breaths watching our cash cow wobbling on its way to the moving truck held high by several strong youths all laughing and grunting with the weight. The move went well. We were in our third year in business and already were in our third location.

The benefit of being right on Mexico's main and only highway was apparent (even though in those days it was only a two lane road). We had some highway signs made and placed them in front of the little access road off the highway indicating our bakery's new location. We still weren't ready for a sit-down retail establishment but no sooner did the signs go out, than the customers started to come, ready or not.

We now had two ovens with a combined capacity of 32 pies! We asked our newest employee, who lived in Bucerias, to find two more women to add to our staff. This she did immediately, and soon we transformed the downstairs of the guesthouse into a real bakery with five women, some now experienced, some still in training. We had developed some new recipes, cookies, pecan tarts and cheesecake tarts made in fluted French tart tins. The tarts made it easier for many as they didn't have to buy a whole pie. Perfect for retail, and soon a big hit. Tarts were more profitable, as we could get more from the recipe. We now had a frosted chocolate layer cake; chocolate, *Kahlúa*, and

Grand Marnier cheesecakes and tarts; pecan pie and tarts; and chocolate chip cookies.

We needed to add an old American favorite, a brownie. Experimenting and gaining weight in the process, we came up with something special that we thought would be a winner, only to somehow lose the recipe during the move. Back to the drawing board. What came out of our twentieth attempt to create the best brownie ever became our signature dessert.

The BESO, (kiss in Spanish), was a round brownie with a molten fudge center. It was an immediate hit, we soon began hearing beso stories. We placed the *beso* on a paper doily and wrapped it in clear, crinkly cellophane tied with a red ribbon. The Beso sported a very inviting gold and red label, featuring a pair of puckered red lips. People traveling up or down the coast, returning to their homes in

Guadalajara would stop by and buy dozens as there just wasn't anything like it anywhere in all of Mexico. A cruiser friend of ours, Scott, used one as a gift to a grumpy customs agent over in the Baja in order to get some marine parts he had sent down, but were being held behind the closed door. He kept coming back whenever the agent told him to come back tomorrow. Something we all heard which translated into "you poor schmuck, you will never get your part without paying something extra". Keeping his cool on his fourth return, Scott placed the packaged beso, in all its glory, on the counter, crinkling the wrapper with his fingers .The customs man, just couldn't stand it any longer and finally asked our friend, what was that he had there? Our friend explained that it was a Beso from Pie-in-the-Sky. The agent, noncommittal, turned and disappeared without a word and returned minutes later with the part. Done! Beso

Power! We also had Mexican women, poor cleaning women, come to buy one for their husbands... touching.

When we first started, we thought that our business would cater mainly to gringos, tourists, and ex-pats, but we were seeing that 80% of our business was local, a big pleasant surprise. We continued to grow and after a couple of years in our guesthouse/bakery we started to look for something larger, with room for retail and a place for clients to sit, have a coffee and a dessert. Walking each morning before the sun came over the hills, and before the workday, we looked for such a place.

Karen's Place in Bucerias

One place that we saw on our walks was in disrepair and obviously vacant. It was located in the south end of Bucerias. This house with the red roof tiles and white walls of an old-style adobe building appealed to us immediately. It sat on a slight hillock, about an acre of land on the main road, but because of its slight elevation, was above the noise of the street. The house was surrounded by a seven foot high white wall crumbling with neglect. We discovered that it was owned by a Mexican guy who lived in Colorado, and were pleasantly surprised that the wife of the owner was an American. As it turned out we had met this woman three years before. We had answered her plea to take her out to her boat which was anchored in front of the Puerto Vallarta naval base. We were rowing back from shopping to the *Galatea*, also anchored nearby, when we heard her calls. When we phoned for info on the Bucerias house Karen answered and remembered us, and our kindness of that day. The house had sat for a couple of years, vacant and exposed to the elements without a caretaker, and they had no plans for it.

"Yes", she said, "we can work something out". We did, and had a lease for a realistic amount. We began the renovations to turn this hacienda into a commercial bakery, coffee, and dessert place. Still operating on a shoestring, we were able to make the move, again with the help of the La Cruz fisherman/ballplayers. We had the surrounding wall repaired and painted white. We had had such success with our first road signs that we thought the wall, with its terrific exposure, was a gift that should be utilized to the fullest extent, but didn't have an idea of what should go there. While making deliveries one day we spotted a small mural that was really well done right on the front of a tropical juices and ice cream shop tucked into the corner of one of the first malls in Vallarta. We asked the employees who the artist was and finally, after three trips back to ask patiently again, got his name and just the name of the town where he lived. It was a start.

Near Puerto Vallarta, and created by its recent growth, was the small settlement of Pitallal, and it was there, after two weeks of searching, we found Juan, the artist. He lived beneath the main power lines in a ramshackle house of cardboard, old scraps of lumber, and rusty roofing material. He was however in good spirits and willing to come out and have a look at this potential canvas.

When we had been in La Cruz starting out, a woman mailed a small painting to us, as a gift. She said that she had been moved by our efforts and lifestyle. The painting was entitled,

"Cherry Pie in Outer space" and it showed a slice of cherry pie flying, as a magic carpet would, with a fox wearing goggles and a raffish scarf flying behind him in the breeze, standing heroically in the middle.

On the pointy end of the pie sat a small cat also with a scarf. The two were flying between and amongst the planets, some with rings and their own moons and stars. Comets painted long arching tails. Sky blue was the main color. We asked Juan if he thought he could use this theme and extend it to 150 feet of wall that was exposed to the main highway. Juan smiled for the first time since meeting us.

After buying all that he needed we set him loose to use his God-given talents as he saw fit. Our new mural which we loved turned out to be not only fantastic, but also the talk of the town.

Entering the high double wooden door entryway through our wall and into the compound the first thing you saw was a ratty looking, non functioning swimming pool. The bottom of this was filled with a few feet of green scummy water. The plumbing and machinery to run the pool system was beyond repair, so all we had was this mosquito breeding hole in the ground. We had hired a general handyman/gardener, Paco, to help us settle in and brighten the place with new grass, plants, and to clean out, seal, and paint the pool. We filled it with fresh water, added a small air pump to keep it moving and clean, and added several fingerling koi fish, purchased at a Puerto Vallarta pet store. Paco then added some water lilies and hyacinths and we had a fishpond.

Our dear friend Katie Ottesen suggested we

needed some exotic banana plants for the grounds and that she knew where to find them. Off we went with Katie driving north to San Blas where she introduced us to two brothers she had known for some time. Katie was nearly 80 and full of life. She was an accomplished artist, world traveler, gourmet cook and fantastic gardener. It was the gardening part that had led her to the brothers. They were surfers and after a season surfing in Indonesia, brought back many exotic fruit seeds which they planted there in the fertile earth of San Blas. By the time we visited, their plantation included jack fruit trees, leechies, star fruit, many varieties of mango, and what we were looking for, Indonesian Blue Banana plants. We were gifted several young plants which we planted later that same day. The trees grew much taller than the local variety and their fruit was indeed blue as it matured, then finally turned yellow just before harvest. The fruit itself tasted like custard with a slight hint of lime. A terrific choice made by our friend. The trees also provided much shade around the grounds and the sit-down space we were creating.

The brothers went on to create a commercial shrimp raising operation in partnership with investors from Thailand. They called their company Ti – Mex and were very successful; although we later heard that they had problems with the government. Such were the inherent problems associated with trying to make a big business in Mexico; there were always *problemas*.

Over the next months we fixed the wraparound porch and added tables and chairs beneath the tall banana palms, a refrigerated display counter, espresso machine, and we had our first retail/coffee/dessert spot. Still turning out pies for our wholesale clients we now watched our retail sales soar, and soon it would earn for us as much as our base wholesale business. This location, our fourth, turned out to be our flagship and the one we still remember as our real bakery.

There was a small apartment on the second floor with its own balcony overlooking the bay and the mountains to the south. We moved the boat to a berth in Nuevo Vallarta, 15 minutes away, so as not to be worried about our boat at anchor, unattended in La Cruz. Our first place with air-conditioning in the bedroom and we really slept well.

We met an American ex-pat who owned a popular convenience store/deli in the new Puerto Vallarta marina complex. He thought that our Besos, which didn't need refrigeration, could be displayed and sold at his store right next to the cash register. With the exposure there, in this new modern marina, we began to be of interest to other point-of-sale locations. This opened a new market for us and soon small popular places had a basketful of our individual treats - Besos and Chocolate Chip Cookies - all over town. No longer halfway legal, we were free to be open about selling and began to trade radio advertising for future gift packages that the station wanted to give out at Christmas. One ad featured a woman's voice asking for a Beso, when the guy, surprised, responds, 'Oh with much pleasure!' She cuts him short and says 'not that kind of beso! A Beso from Pie in the Sky'. Cute, fun and very popular!

We soon opened our own retail place with coffee and tables in the old town section of

PV on what was called "The Street of Cafés". The day we signed the lease "The Street of Cafes" was torn up! Every cobblestone was taken up to be replaced with a modern surface. It took six months to reopen but by then all the locals knew that we were there as well as 15 miles north in Bucerias. As soon as we signed the lease for this new location we hired Juan to do his magic on the outside wall and so, his and our reputations received new southern exposure.

We hired a guy to build what we referred to as, "an aromas tube" on the roof of our new store. We wanted the chocolate beso aromas from our baking oven to be blown by the fan through the tube out onto the street and draw people in. Overnight "The Street of Cafés" quickly became the Street of Chocolate.

Shortly after its complicated assembly, and

functioning very well for less than a week, we received a visit from a good client who owned and ran a very popular restaurant, two doors away from our store. He complained that he was trying to sell his customers lobsters and steaks, but all anyone could smell was chocolate cake! We shut it down, thus keeping the peace and his business.

Having a satellite location required a certain amount of faith from us, being almost absentee owners, trusting to whoever ran the place. We received reports that Adelina's husband was allowing a naked kid to run wild in the store during working hours. Another time, a young employee who was clearly stealing, and once fired, turned and tried to sue. Mexico has laws that put the burden of social care etc. heavily on the businesses. If you hire a local, after one day, if you fire them, you must give them three months pay.

We had a local lawyer who helped, as did our accountant, whose day job was as owner of the local paint store. Usually our loyal staff kept all employees honest. When we needed to hire another person our senior girls would show up with just the right person in tow, ready to learn. Where were all these quality, honest and enthusiastic women coming from, we wondered. Everyone we knew had horror stories about Mexican employees but we were almost unscathed. At Christmas we received our answer.

We arranged to take over a quarter of a client's restaurant for a Christmas party, our first. When only two couples showed up we were not only amazed but very disappointed. We now had several employees all of whom had been asked to bring husband, boyfriend, and children. Our Catholic employee, Yasmin, let us in on what was happening. Unbeknown to us, the no-shows were all Jehovah's Witnesses. Upon looking into more of that religion's beliefs, we learned that they do not celebrate Christmas, nor do they party. They are however, and more importantly, honest and hard-working and make for very loyal employees.

The following Christmas season we masked the party as an "office business meeting" held again at our friend and client's restaurant. We finally had our full group attending, enjoying, even dancing and drinking at what we continued to refer to as a "business meeting". This also explained how easy it was for our employees to show up right away with someone new to train. They had all come from the same group. One problem we couldn't overcome however, were the jealousies a few of the husbands felt because their wives were making more money than they were. We did lose a couple of really good workers because of that.

After a year of success with our "Street of Cafés" store, we opened the second store on the other side of town, and we felt that we had P.V. covered. Business was good, still growing, but anything we made was being spent on new employees. We didn't care as long as we had enough to at least cover a long low-season. We thought as long as our overhead was met, that our personal income would come to us whenever we sold the business. It was much more important that we continue to add employees so that we could be free to spend more time on our boat and enjoy all that Mexico had to offer.

We had a well-trained, loyal, honest and hard-working team and we couldn't afford to lose any of them even through the low season, or as some locals called it the time of seven hungers. So although Christmas through Easter was banner months for us, the summer was bleak. We had to continue to come up with new products to entice those who had not been tempted yet.

We were now in our fifth year of business and were spending less and less time at the bakery. Our girls were all working smoothly together. Our driver/delivery guy, Martin, fit right in without any macho displays towards them and they in turn helped him get all the orders for the day's delivery packed and loaded into the delivery truck. This was all done with much laughter and joking. We had hired a local woman to run the office and take care of the day-to-day accounting and banking. Our retail section was now busy with espresso-making and the serving and the selling of tarts. This was handled by whoever wasn't in the middle of a run at the time. With all these recent changes, the bakery took on a new rhythm and pace. People loved hanging out eating our desserts beneath the palms and next to the koi pond with its water lilies and hyacinths.

The koi were fed daily, and with the absence of commercial fish food, we substituted Friskies' fish recipe dry cat food, much to their delight and our cat's interest. It turned out that along with our cat, Paco also had an interest! Seeing how fast and how big the Koi population had grown, the first generation now almost a foot long. Unbeknownst to us, Paco, surreptiously had introduced river crayfish into the mix!

One morning while casting Friskies across the surface of the pond, a large, fast, dark shape, shot up from beneath the cover of lily pads, and just as quickly, disappeared! "What the hell?" Word spread quickly that something was very strange in the Koi realm and I noticed all the women were looking at an area of the garden where Paco was working. He had to fess up eventually and promised to build a trap to catch all the crayfish. He thought there were so many fish that he hoped the crayfish would grow fat and multiply so he'd have something to sell on the side.

Yes, these were quite the years for the Pie in the Sky Bakery. We had been initially hesitant to move to Bucerias in the first place, giving up our more peaceful lifestyle in La Cruz. After our disastrous experience on the Calle de Cafes in Puerto Vallarta proper, we were lucky to be in Karen's place right on the main road of the west coast of Mexico. Being there more than paid off for us and our commercial desires. We settled in for the next five years and really enjoyed being in Bucerias with its simple seafood restaurants right on the beach. The Beso got invented and Katie introduced us to the Thai Fruit/Shrimp pioneers up the coast. We will always be inspired by our friend Katie, her chutzpah and her adventuresome years in her 80s. What a gal!

They were heady days, long gone now that things have changed so much in Mexico.

CHAPTER 5

Freedom, Loss and the Power of Intention

Placentia, Belize

Due to the success of our newly expanded location in Bucerias we had more time to ourselves and playing hooky became a daily occurrence.

We did some of our best sailing during this time, and also started to take road trips exploring more of Mexico. In the summer, we left the baking to continue operating with the team in charge who, by then, we had complete confidence in. Our trips were short at first, with many phone calls from us, each call was met with the "all's okay here" reply and "have a good time" response. We felt we had it made... and we had!

We traveled in the off season, just after Easter until the beginning of July. July and August are the vacation months for Mexicans and they loved stopping at our bakery first to gather all the unique treats that we offered.

One trip we took was driving our older 4x4 Suburban from the bakery all the way through Mexico to southern Belize. We passed through Mexico City on the way there and through the state of Chiapas, the ancient Mayan ceremonial center of Palenque, and the fabulous old marketplaces of Oaxaca on the return.

We had agreed to meet a couple of friends from Sausalito, Ken and Elizabeth of the *Becky Thatcher* houseboat. We stayed with them in their magical place, on our trips to Sausalito and San Francisco. Now we had decided on Placentia at the southern end of Belize, to be our vacation spot. After we drove for five days, across Mexico, and into Belize, we arrived at the airport in Belize City a half hour before their plane landed! What timing!

The one road south to Placencia was a washboard of crushed coral and shell. We found it impossible to find a slow enough speed to allow us to continue. An expat who had hitched a ride south with us told us that most people found that it smoothed out above 50 mph! That did the trick and we glided into Placencia. The place was then a local hamlet, the end of the line in the south, where few tourists ventured. Francis Ford Coppola hadn't yet discovered Placencia where he later built a luxury resort. Further west laid low mountains which contained many Mayan ruins that did draw tourists. The four of us enjoyed our time there and later toured the Cays to the north, Cay Caulker, especially. We returned Ken and Elizabeth to Belize City to catch their flight back to California and then traveled north to the Yucatán and the colonial town of Merida. We met my son Brad there as planned and he came with us on our long road trip back to the bakery. Our trip brought us through "Maya" land, jungles, mountains, waterfalls, beaches, and finally back to the Pie in the Sky Bakery and our wonderful Banderas Bay.

Although we were on a tight schedule to meet Brad at his flight's arrival in Merida, we had to get our shocks fixed or replaced. All four shock absorbers on this high clearance, four-wheel drive, go-almost-anywhere Suburban, were completely gone. They were actually hanging loose and nonfunctional after the torture of traveling over the washboard surface of the Placencia road. The car rode like a pony on a merry-go-round, all over the road.

We had to do something but the chances of finding a parts store that would even carry old Chevy parts much less be open on a Sunday seemed nil. As we rounded a bend in the highway a giant sign loomed on top of a commercial building, stating in large Spanish letters, "Miracle of God Truck Repair." Honest, we couldn't make that up. God's miracle was open on Sunday and going full tilt! Our oversized station wagon seemed like a kid's toy next to what was being worked on there that day. The owner/manager took pity on us and assigned a young apprentice to handle our mess. Two hours, and a lunch in a nearby cantina later, and our car was ready. The shocks had been cut from the frame, disassembled, repaired, reassembled and welded back in place for $25!

We met my son on time and traveled to the magical and mysterious Mayan Ruins of Palenque in Chiapas. I looked up a Mexican stone carver friend I had met there a dozen years earlier, who acted as our guide. Roberto Cruz had developed into a master carver in the years since we had last met. He copied the Stellas so prominently displayed on many of the temples walls of Palenque. He worked in sandstone and sold his precise and beautiful work to the tourists.

On the road to Oaxaca we stopped often by the jungle, to explore pools and cascades, and to jump off rocks into waterfall pools. We spent many lovely hours sitting in or by some form of water, in the jungle, listening to and looking at the most fabulous birds and butterflies.

Oaxaca was not the political hotspot it became shortly after our visit. Commander Marcos, the pipe smoking, masked revolutionary leader, hadn't made his presence known. When he did, however, as the leader of the Indian insurrection, their uprising caused tens of thousands of troops to arrive and camp out throughout the area.

The three of us drove down the mountainous roads to the Pacific coast and the towns of Puerto Angel and Huatulco. We were lucky to have seen it on that trip. This was before the government stepped in and began relocating people living along the beaches to inland sites miles from the coast. The ones who complained long enough or were connected in some way were allowed to buy taxi permits or marine permits to take tourists out fishing. This wholesale relocation was the first step in opening up the pristine coast to make room for the big boys and their resorts and planned communities.

We returned to the bakery almost one month after we left. We were beside ourselves with joy at the notion we could travel and the business could run as if we had been there.

Losing the *Galatea*

During our time traveling we kept our boat tied to a dock behind a private house in Nuevo Vallarta. The water there was swamplike and growth had fouled the bottom of the boat, and more importantly the prop. When we returned we started the motor and attempted to motor the boat over to the clean waters of La Cruz so I could dive on the bottom and clean it. The boat refused to budge. The growth on the prop rendered it absolutely useless. Picture a football spinning in the water. There being no wind at all to sail, a problem only in the summer when it was often hot and muggy, we just had to wait. So it was during this time of waiting for a break in our work and a day with some wind that we became aware that hurricane "Rosa" was moving up the coast.

"R", indicates that 18 other named storms had preceded already, this being November. November is normally a hurricane-free month. "Rosa" wasn't expected to cause any more than heavy rains in our area. Hurricanes very seldom entered Banderas Bay when traveling up the west coast of southern Mexico. This was due to the mountain range behind Yelapa which carried their height west to Cabo Corrientes, at the southern entrance of the Bay. The storms would normally pass by the entrance to the Bay and continue north to Mazatlan or over to the Baja where they had hit many times. Puerto Vallarta and the Bay hadn't had a hurricane for over 50 years.

When a windy day did arrive we sailed out of our hole and up to La Cruz, where we would fix our simple prop problem. We arrived at night and anchored into the sandy bottom there. My air tank was empty and the next day dawned with me running into town to get it filled. The morning sky was an ominous green and black.

Hurricane Rosa had advanced to just outside the Bay. Instead of continuing her northerly path, Rosa made a turn that targeted our safe haven. There wasn't time to do the bottom. We were in "the calm before the storm" - scorching hot and muggy with no movement of air. The black sky, turning more dark green by the hour, prompted us to prepare for the worst, right where we sat at anchor.

The protection of the breakwater couldn't help us due to a large sailing yacht having already taken up a position there, with lines crisscrossing the small harbor. I thought that we might lose the *Galatea* in this blow but I didn't want to be responsible for damaging this other yacht. So we placed our other two anchors, one of which was very heavy, with all the chain and line we had, outside the breakwater, in open shallow water off La Cruz. We cleared the decks and made sure all was battened down tight. When the first winds and seas began that late afternoon I felt

I had done everything possible, under the condition. Wishing her well, I returned to the bakery.

Rosa with winds over 100 mph, did enter the Bay, and when the first heavy winds hit our building we walked out on the porch only to be pushed by the wind to the back wall. It was if a large hand pressed on our chests and moved us back. I felt then that we had lost our girl. Throughout the night with power lines and poles down, trees falling across the roads, roof tiles and coconuts flying through the air and crashing, we both feared the worst. At first light we managed to skirt the problem areas of the main road, and made it to La Cruz and the beach.

No *Galatea*!
Our hearts stopped. Martin, our friend and delivery guy, came up with a few other

fisherman to offer their condolences, saying that there was nothing that they could have done to save our boat. The waves hitting that shallow water off the anchorage had simply picked up our boat, breaking her hold on the bottom, and pushed her toward Bucerias and the rocks. We made it there and looked out on one of the saddest scenes of my life. Pieces of our boat were scattered down the coast. Sails and lines swirling in the surf.
The mast, boom, and gaff… all gone.

The transom with her name and port was still whole but it was no longer attached to the hull and deck, the cabin top was gone, revealing parts of the cabinetry down below. Gone, gone!

People began to gather to see if they could begin to salvage anything useful. We were so crushed we could hardly speak but we gave them permission to gather anything they could use and left.

It took us two years to be able to return to that very spot. When we finally did, Teri and I held a belated wake, in the middle of which we realized that we were standing on top of her keel - almost totally hidden in the sand!

I felt that I was responsible for her loss and that somehow there were things I could have done to keep her from this cruel fate.

But it was done and we can only learn from our mistakes. In later years we took hurricanes more seriously and in one case, on another boat of ours, the *Sonador*, in Carriacou in the southern Caribbean, sat securely in the mangroves while two hurricanes, Earl and Ivan, roared over our heads as we baked cookies. The two hurricanes were two weeks apart.

Our new friends, Coco and Twiggy Quijano, offered us their boat when they weren't using it. They lived in Mexico City where they owned a horse jumping club, and seldom used their boat. Theirs was a 38-foot sloop, larger and more modern than the *Galatea* for us to use anytime we wished. It was berthed behind the same house where we had kept the *Galatea*. So although we lost our lovely girl we were still sailing on the Bay.

Selling the Bakery and the Devaluation

After a few more years at Pie in the Sky Bakery, President Salinas, as as he was going out of office, devalued the peso, quite unexpectedly a couple of days just before

Christmas 1995. We had tired of the business by then and were ready to sell it and continue to cruise with a new boat. We had advertised the bakery for sale and a family from Leon, Mexico had shown serious interest in buying it. In early December we were in the process of dickering with them when the devaluation blindsided us.

The Salinas devaluation changed everything overnight. Instantly our bakery was worth one half of what it had been a few days earlier. If our business had been dealing in dollars instead of pesos or had dollars in the bank, it would have been an advantage. That not being the case made it difficult to continue.

During this time the price of ingredients skyrocketed beyond comprehension. Employees needed more to get by and services went up as well. Only sales went down. We were forced to raise our already high prices to loyal restaurant clients who were staggered by this drastic change. It was hard to do but we had to do it. Several price adjustments later we were still operating but it took us three years to regain our financial position to justify our original sales price.

We were also under pressure to start making short cuts with our recipes, but we held our ground and just raised our prices to allow us to continue to get the best ingredients at three times what we had been paying before.

Right after the devaluation, during a meeting with our attorney, he gave us his opinion on how we might continue our growth, even in this bad economy. His idea. . . "Franchise Pie in the Sky"!

Never a big fan of franchises, still we could see the benefits to our Pie in the Sky concept. Franchisees, once chosen, must come up with an initial fee plus a monthly percentage of their sales, both of which were something we could badly use. Back in '95 the Mexican laws governing franchising within Mexico were quite easy to satisfy. The stricter rules in the United States would have required us to take on partners just to be able to afford to meet their requirements. After quite a bit of thought and local research, we decided to jump into the game and create a franchise, with a training manual, recipes, retail/wholesale guides, training, and our services including help with site selection. What a big job.

Our Pie in the Sky Bakery Franchise website was advertising the franchise in English and Spanish and so we received inquiries from all over the world, more and more each week. After a few weeks of having it up, if you typed in "bakery franchise", we would come up number one on the Alta Vista search engine. What a thrill to hear from the Canary Islands and Guayaquil, Ecuador.

Our first franchise was in Guadalajara. We were very proud to have it there in Mexico's second largest city and with a very prestigious family. And because of it and the newly formed NAFTA (Northern American Free Trade Agreement- between the U.S., Mexico and Canada) we became the rags-to-riches story featured in their "Voice of NAFTA Magazine". We received a call from a friend of Teri's dad, a lawyer, who said he was very interested in what we were doing. He flew down and laid out his idea. As an International lawyer, he specialized in immigration and investments for Filipinos.

He said he could send us as many qualified franchisees as we could train, only if we had permission in the States to franchise. Purchasing and operating a Pie in the Sky Franchise would enable his clients to gain a certain immigration status and a way to start a business in the U.S. There it was, someone we could trust, and all the business we could want.

However, we came to realize that by continuing to do franchises we'd have to commit our full time attention to the business that would end up being more like what we had set sail to escape, eleven years earlier. No thanks!

We began to put more energy into selling Pie in the Sky and moving on. We developed another good web site offering our business for sale. During this time we were negotiating for a second franchise - one in Cabo San

Lucas area on the Baja. A couple from Fairbanks had kept us hopping back and forth looking for locations, etc., but it never amounted to anything.

One day a friend was looking over my shoulder while I was working on the website and read the ad and exclaimed that she hadn't realized it before but she and her husband would be perfect to buy and continue Pie in the Sky.

So after fielding many inquiries from all over the world, we finally ended up selling to a couple from Oakland, Phil and Susan, who were building their retirement home 30 minutes drive west from Bucerias. Talk about the power of intention! They continue owning and successfully running the bakery 27 years later.

CHAPTER 6

Tonga, Australia and Replenishing the Kitty in Sausalito

Master Franchise - Australia

Several months before we sold the business, we had an inquiry on our franchise website from an English lawyer living in Australia who wanted to know if an Australian/New Zealand master franchise might be possible.

At the time, it certainly was, and we had lots of back and forth. He claimed to have been a lawyer for Kentucky Fried Chicken in Europe at one time. Nothing developed, but when we sold the business we told him that we were headed in his direction and would look him up when we were in Australia. We wanted to fly through the South Pacific, making stops along the way, Tonga, Fiji, New Zealand, and finally Australia where we planned to look for another sailboat. Fresh off the business, we were still alert for business opportunities and when in Tonga set to investigate the world of kava, a medicinal root locally grown and very popular in health food stores in the States at the time.

The markets in Tonga were a sad affair, especially after the cornucopia of colorful and healthy fruits and produce laid out in a typical Mexican market. Roots and tubers appeared to be the main staple, along with Spam, which was really favored by the men. We bought

several samples of kava at the market, trying
them all. We were led to the one kava broker
on the island and got to try kava from other
islands, including Fiji. They didn't do anything
for us that we could tell; we were already
pretty loose.

Disappointed in the kava, we then moved
quickly through the possibilities of vanilla,
more appealing than kava but requiring the
same amount of attention if we were to begin
another business just then. We flew from the
North Island down to the capital in the South.

The King of Tonga's palace was within
walking distance where we were staying, and
after seeing him giving out medals to the
rugby team on the room's TV, Teri noticed
that his movements weren't right. A very large
man, he was favoring one leg or hip. Teri was
off the next morning with me in tow, to offer

her acupuncture expertise to the King.

Even though it was an early Sunday morning, the soldier at the main gate pointed us to a low compound of several small buildings and garages and told us to tell our story there, Teri was encouraged. The wooden three story palace, right out of the tales of the South Pacific and the 1800s, was on one side of the grounds and the service buildings on the other. As we approached we saw a couple of soldiers standing and talking beside a van whose side door was open and we walked up to them for directions. The two were very startled by our presence and started talking animatedly, in what could only later be describe as "talking in tongues." As we paid attention to the closest one and his flailing around, we saw inside the van, and there lying on top of old clothes and food wrappers, were automatic weapons, empty beer bottles, and a bottle of local whiskey.

We both sensed that this was not the place to be at that moment and while casually backing up, we claimed that tomorrow would probably be better. We had found the king's soldiers very altered on more than a couple of beers. Tonga would have been better viewed and experienced from a boat at anchor than what we saw of it from land.

We visited New Zealand and loved it and our experiences there, with the exception of having to drive defensively among very competitive Kiwi drivers in a rental car whose steering wheel was on the "wrong side". When approaching a roundabout even when we planned our exit it seemed all hell would break loose.

We spent a few days in Auckland's great

international restaurants living large after being hicks from coastal Mexico for so long. We took a trip south to the coastal town of Tauranga, a town on the Bay of Plenty. This beautiful town is noted for its maritime flavor, including a large marina with several yacht brokerages. We booked into a B and B. The only guests, we were treated royally by the owners. They had a small farm where they raised sheep. It was late afternoon when we arrived and as soon as we were showered and changed, we were directed to the local pub. This was our first time in a local and it must have showed because we were welcomed as strangers and sailors right away. Many rounds later, all drunk while standing around a shared table, one of the regulars, a fisherman, pulled out a bag of pot, and began to roll a spliff right there. Our grins belied our amazement. Outside half the crowd with us in tow, moseyed to an area outside the kitchen door, where we all shared. Back inside, while enjoying some munchies with our drinks, we realized that the pub was actually divided in half. Nothing structural, but the half we were standing in was occupied with white locals, while the other was all Maori. Hard to tell at first glance, but as we focused on the group as a whole we could see the separation.

We walked around for a while and settled in at a round table where several Maori were drinking and laughing, both men and women. A little cool to us at first, they soon softened and became more welcoming once they heard we had just arrived from 12 years in Mexico and that we were sailors and fishermen. We bought a round and they offered us a treat just outside. Curious, we followed them outside and right over to the same smoking spot behind the kitchen we had just used with the others. We had a chance to taste test the samplings offered by the two groups; both did the job.

The next morning we were in our host's dining room having the best breakfast we had had in years. We were talking with the woman of the house when her husband entered and joined us for a cup of coffee. The first thing he said was, "Ah - - I heard you were with some of the wild ones last night, smoking the wickey-wacky weed at the local". It was only 7:30 in the morning and our host had just returned from a trip to town and he already knew it all. He went on in an entertaining way, to tell us who it was that we had been drinking with, by name, occupation and reputation. We later visited some of these "wild ones" at their work, especially the fishermen and sailors who continued their hospitality toward us. They showed us around the waterfront and introduced us to a broker they all knew and liked. Many enjoyable hours we spent walking that waterfront, looking at lots of boats for sale and meeting the very friendly locals.

The Cormandel peninsula, just above Tauranga, is noted for three things: its Big Sur-like geography and coast, the fine local pot, and the green lipped mussels farmed in the waters there. We loved it all, especially the mussels, we couldn't get our fill.

Vowing to return soon for more of the same and to explore the South Island we flew on to Australia's Queensland; Brisbane and our English lawyer. He and his Indian wife and their children lived on the outskirts of Brisbane in some nice horse country.

We spent time together over the next couple of weeks and then agreed to start an Australian corporation and run it more or less as we had done in Mexico, only refining the production down to a single dessert. The "Beso" was the choice to go with and we set about starting a 'Third World' Beso test kitchen in a 'First World 'residential neighborhood. First though, we bought a boat.

The 15-foot power boat we found was small, strongly built of welded aluminum and had a center steering console with a recent outboard motor. We bought it from a Kiwi fisherman, obsessed with fishing, who showed us album after album of fish he had caught with that boat. He would tow it behind an old four wheel drive flat bed truck and launch it in the surf, alone! We trailed it behind our old four-cylinder Volvo station wagon. We'd launch it nearby, and race the River Cats, very large commercial passenger ferries into and beyond Brisbane city center, great fun in between training the new girls to work in the factory.

Every day before sunset, we'd walk down by the Brisbane River that flowed through the University grounds. Sitting on a dock we'd witness the evening parade of fruit bats flying, swooping over the river to the parks with fruit trees in the city. Every sunset they'd come by the thousands. These bats have a wingspan of over three feet! One day while puttering around the river in our boat we encountered some of the early flyers and continued up river until we found the home base of these creatures. Trees along the river's edge hosted hundreds of bats per tree, all hanging upside down, wings wrapping their bodies like Bela Lugosi's cape.

We started the test kitchen in the lower-level of a house that we leased in St Lucia, a lovely suburb adjacent to the Queensland University, and its beautiful campus on the Brisbane River. We located a used Blodgett oven, our old favorite work horse, and had to hire a modern, mobile crane with crew to lift it over the house and down the other side, a full story below street level. A crew of waiting hands with dollies and expertise helped us move it with ease into our new test kitchen – a far cry from the La Cruz baseball club. We hired part-time University of Queensland students, one Chinese, one Vietnamese, and worked with them, and through their ethnic differences and ancient animosities, to crank out our quality product and test the market. As it turned out, everyone loved the *Beso*, but wouldn't pay the price. We hired a sales team and began wholesaling to shops, stores, restaurants, and cafés, most were owned and operated by Italians or Greeks. We changed the size and tried a different market, but the long and short of it was that in trying to make it big in the 'First World' and flush with success from our Mexican adventure, we ventured on, spending all we had made from the sale of Pie in the Sky Bakery. Twelve years of work in the 'Third World', blown on a business idea in the 'First World' in six months.

The original business plan showed us making much more and much faster than reality. We didn't want to go into debt just to become bakers and businessmen again so we cut our losses and with our tails tucked, returned to Sausalito to replenish the "cruising kitty". Now that we were broke again we knew we'd have to find a way to make money and quickly.

Several weeks before we shut down and left Australia, we sold the La Cruz property, online. We knew the fellow who bought the land, and had shown it to him while we were still in Mexico. We had given up on him even though he said he'd be back. Well, he did get back, and just before we were absolutely broke, and just before leaving, we were flush once again.

The pressure of having to find some way to earn good old US dollars right away was off. We decided to check out places other than Sausalito, to set up as a base until we could afford to leave again. As pretty as she is, Sausalito had changed a lot in the previous 13 years. The old waterfront, with its unique and very funky houseboat communities had, for the most part, been cleaned up. Houseboats sold for as much as a Marin County home. There were a few diehard groups, however, and that's where all our friends lived.

We visited our old friend Alex, an ex-partner

of mine from the *Sailing Connection* days, who lived in Seattle. Alex had always wanted us to move up to the Pacific Northwest saying that since we love the water so much we would absolutely fall in love with this area just south of the Canadian Border. It was the end of winter and beautiful, but after 13 years of living in tropical environments; it seemed bone chilling cold and uncomfortable to us. We crossed Seattle and Puget Sound off the list as very beautiful, but too cold to consider. It's funny how things change.

In December 1999 we returned to Sausalito and rented a room in a hilltop house for $1000 a month, for a room with a bath, nothing more! The reality of the U.S. economy as compared with our experience in Mexico shocked us. If we were going to live and work from here, we would have to find a boat and a live-aboard berth. We had lots of friends who were anchored out, but we couldn't both work and do that. An old friend, Bridget from the Gate 3 community, on the Sausalito waterfront, and more recently, La Paz in the Baja, heard that we were back in town and without a boat. She was on her way back to Mexico and offered to rent us her houseboat in Galilee Harbor on the edge of downtown. Galilee harbor, a nonprofit co-op, was a collection of 40 to 50 houseboats, all of eclectic design and construction. I knew most of those there from my days with the Sailing Connection, a Sausalito company I started some years before, and later on as a fisherman, based at gate 3, and living on a houseboat there.

The Galilee Houseboat Community was made up of a bunch of waterfront characters, overflowing with talent and creativity, and as their nonprofit charter decreed, "of marine-based occupations," fisherman, boat builders, sailing captains, sail makers, merchant seaman, their wives, girlfriends, and families all living in close harmony while fighting for their very existence. The town and county both wanted us out. Thanks to the support and guidance of a County Supervisor, who was one of us, we managed to skirt disasters, meet standards required by oh so many agencies, and finally win out.

While we were renting Bridget's houseboat another boat in the harbor came up for sale, a converted double-ended lifeboat. A bit top heavy with the sleeping loft, especially in a good blow, but comfy aboard. We had been approved by the community as new members, and welcomed in our new boat. I was voted in as a board member. We had everything we needed to begin replenishing the kitty.

Teri had been brought up to date on the latest acupuncture and alternative health scene by her long time friend Jennifer, who she had gone to acupuncture school with in England. Teri had kept her California license as 'inactive' so after taking the necessary credit classes to meet educational requirement she was reinstated as 'active' once again. Teri quickly allied herself with a group of Worsley acupuncturists she had gone to school with in the 70's. She shared an office and treatment room in both a stylish practice in Mill Valley and an opulent office on Union Street in San Francisco.

Word of Teri's return to practice in Mill Valley soon turned up old patients anxious to be treated again by her and hear of her travels and adventures of the last twelve years. I rebuilt our just purchased, funky old houseboat into such a gem inside that my son named it a geode - ugly on the outside, beautiful in the middle. I was thinking of doing some type of sailing charter work on the Bay, so I studied and passed the Coast Guard exams and received my 50 Ton Coast Guard Master's license. This was necessary as I was looking for water-based opportunities only.

Someone told me that the Sea Ray Yacht dealer in the Bay Area was looking for yacht salesman with experience. I went over to Oakland to talk to the manager and came away with the job. Surprising really, seeing as my real reported work history was pretty much nonexistent, that, plus the fact that I was in my mid-60s, and the oldest Sea Ray salesman in California. Working in the world of jackets and ties again, although surreal, was very profitable, and soon I was one of their top earners.

Driving Teri to her office at 8:30 a.m., crossing the bridge to Oakland on a very scary freeway was a sobering reality check: here we were connecting again in this insane world, with its traffic and attitude... "Gees" we both thought, "let's get out of here as soon as possible."

After about a year, Teri's health began to suffer from the cold and damp of northern waterfront living. She needed warmer weather to get well. I arranged for a transfer and soon joined the Stuart, Florida group in Sea Ray's newest showcase on the entire east coast. This quality motor yacht company was building its complex, in Stuart, right on the St. Lucie River, and was minutes away from the Intercoastal Waterway (ICW) and the Atlantic. We bought a small boat and found a co-op apartment right on the river with docks in front, and only a short walk to my office.

After months of waiting, Teri received her Florida acupuncture license and set about beginning yet another practice, this time in a very strange place. Of all the Florida cities on the Atlantic coast, however, Stuart is one of the best, laid back and water oriented. We used our boat to schmooze our way up the St. Lucie River to Lake Okeechobee, and up and down the waterways. Our ocean trips were for fishing and only son Colin was really interested in that. His older brother was just becoming a dad with the recent arrival of his first son and couldn't get away.

Working in Florida was a whole lot different than California, more cutthroat in approach to work and less amenable to working together. After boat shows in the Miami and Fort Lauderdale areas, I was really tired of it and began to count the days till we could leave.

Teri's father lived straight across the state from our east coast to his west, in Cape Coral. We would drive past Lake Okeechobee and the sugar towns to visit him there. His health was failing so it was good to be closer than we had been for a while. He and his loving wife Ruth were our biggest supporters and we miss them dearly. A parent's passing is a sad thing to absorb. We feel lucky that fates were able to put us in Florida so that we could have that one last year with him. After he passed away we left Florida and headed to visit our friends in Trinidad, to look for our next boat and a place to live.

We had, in the year working out of Sausalito, selling the houseboat, and a year working in Stuart, put enough aside to buy a simple cruising sailboat, if we were lucky. Trinidad had the reputation as a good place to find boats on the cheap. My social security kicked in and so we felt free once again. Giving my suits and ties away to the Goodwill and putting on my Tevas, it was off to the southern Caribbean.

CHAPTER 7

Trinidad and Carriacou on Land

Our midnight arrival at the airport in Trinidad coincided with the arrival of contestants and officials belonging to the Miss Universe Contest which was being run in Trinidad by Donald Trump that year. As we adjusted to the heat upon walking to the terminal, we heard the Steel Drums and all of a sudden we found ourselves in a walkway lined on both sides with members of the Carnival! The place was rocking with the very loud music of Trinidad, Moko Jumbies dancing on stilts, fabulous costumes and feathers, and of course the steel drums, it was a welcome unlike any other.

Our friends Jeff and Dawn Stone owned and operated a Marine refrigeration business in the main Marina in Chagaramas, Trinidad. I taught Jeff how to sail many years before in Sausalito. We went on to become great friends and partners in a few fishing ventures and did a lot of sailing together. He and his new wife, Dawn, bought a boat and sailed it through the Pacific to Tahiti then returned to visit with us in Mexico and ended up in Chagaramas, Trinidad after sailing through the Canal and exploring all of the Caribbean. Jeff told us that they had been inspired by what we had done in Mexico, and totally broke, as we had been, started doing what he knew best, marine refrigeration. Their business thrived and Jeff became the go-to-guy in that field. We had been looking forward to seeing them again and seeing what they had developed.

Chagaramas is a marine center and oil supply area in the northwest corner of the island, and is also where many Caribbean cruisers take their boats to avoid the hurricanes and do work on them while waiting for the hurricane season to pass. Many cruisers would do the same in Venezuela but in recent years it had become a very dangerous place, with many reports of deadly attacks on cruisers at anchor. Some of these victims were simply in the way of a drug shipment, in the wrong anchorage at the wrong time.

Trinidad is way at the bottom of the chain of Caribbean islands almost touching the corner of South America. It is nestled by the mouth and delta of Venezuela's Orinoco River and one of the hottest places either of us had ever visited. It was a blast from a furnace hot! Like many of the women there, Teri sometimes had to walk under an umbrella in the daytime just to make it from shade spot to shade spot.

Once we cleared customs and immigration at the airport, we were off on a very wild car ride to the marina and their boat. The main upscale marina in Chagaramas is where Jeff and Dawn kept their boat, an English ketch which would be our home while visiting. We got the full tour from those two and after exploring the boat yards and anchorages, thought this was a great place to do or have done for you cheaply, work on your boat. It was also a great place to find one, used and way below market prices although none we saw on that first visit fit our needs and budget.

Trinidad was very interesting, but we also

wanted to check out the islands of Bequia, part of St. Vincent and the Grenadines, and Carriacou which is part of Grenada. We were, in addition to looking for a boat, looking for a place to stay and these two islands held promise. We flew north and worked our way down through the Grenadines. Bequia was heaven compared with Trinidad, small, very quaint and full of history. Still a whaling port, the local community is allowed a whale or two a year. They use the boats they've been using for hundreds of years; sail and oar only. The island sounded like a great place to base when we first heard about it from our friends Jack and Barbara Thomson who lived there 30 years before. Now it was on the verge of being overdone, tourist-wise.

We took a boat from Bequia over to St Vincent to pay a visit to Mrs. Josephine Nelson, an old friend of Teri's from her teaching days in Chicago. She served us tea and cookies and told us what to look out for as we traveled the various islands. Her close friend, 80-year-old, Mr. Hercules, was our driver, a man as thin as a straw. After exploring Grenada to the south we lit out for Carriacou by fast catamaran ferry.

Carriacou is known as a boat building/fishing/smugglers island and is part of Grenada, but 25 miles and a world away from the Spice Island. The name "Carriacou" means "land surrounded by reefs" and it really does that name justice. The water near the shores of the main island and all the smaller keys is breathtakingly beautiful.

The island is only 8 miles long and its three main settlements, Hillsborough, Windward and Tyrell Bay, are all connected by small passenger "combis" (VW vans) with four rows of shared benches or seats. The ride to anywhere goes through the main waterfront city of Hillsborough, with a customs shed on the only commercial pier. An immigration office; a bank; a two story simple hotel; a few small food shops; a small fish stall with mostly small fish, the post office, and a hardware store rounded out most of Hillsborough's business district, a place where the meat was exceptionally fresh, killed and butchered outside for all to see, an hour before it appeared dressed out in the shop. Of the several thousand inhabitants of the whole island, Hillsboro was host to half. We found it refreshing that Carriacou had neither tourist facilities nor shops catering to them. There were a few day trippers, and few longer term visitors compared to its better known neighbors; it was like turning the clock back 50 years, to the era of wooden trading schooners and open air rum shops.

We booked a room in the town's only hotel and in the morning hopped aboard a combi for a tour of the island. The combis often go off the one lane main road to deliver older passengers right to their door or steps. People would run up and ask the driver to drop off a package to a house along the way. The extreme of that delivery system was when the combi door slid open and a woman stood holding an infant wrapped in a blanket and asked if anyone knew Rita Mae. When a local woman in back said that she did, the woman immediately leaned in and passed the baby back saying "take this baby to she", and the door slammed shut and off we went, the baby still asleep. The sense of community spirit and simple helpfulness was evident right away. Every person on the bus had a grin, laughing and joking, it was amazing. The patois was English, but its Caribbean lilt and local slang left us sensing more than understanding most of what we heard. At the end of that second day on the island, our faces were sore from constantly smiling. One of the combi drivers when asked about safety issues on the island said, "No frights here, Mon". This was a fine place to just be and we loved it right away. We especially liked Tyrell Bay in the south east. It had the only boat yard on the island and a great anchorage that held 40 or more boats at anchor without feeling crowded.

We stayed in what was called the Yacht Club, and after surviving aerial bombardments by mosquitoes all night were out and about early the next morning. We heard from someone at the boat yard that a wooden English built ketch might be for sale and pointed her out. The boat was an old beauty and we met with the Danish owner. The old guy had a drinking problem, but we thought we had an understanding on what the boat was worth and how we would finance it.

While we were trying to arrange for a survey of the Dane's ketch, we received word from our Yelapa pals, Joan and Bryden, now in their summer place in New Mexico, that Bryden had suffered a stroke. Teri was experienced working with stroke victims. After talking with Joan, we decided to fly up to Taos immediately. Teri was intent on treating Bryden as quickly as possible, since early treatment of stroke victims is a critical issue.

Before leaving Carriacou, we met with the owner of the ketch and gave him a deposit to hold the boat until we returned and could have her surveyed. He agreed and took the money.

We had recently visited with Joan and Bryden but hadn't yet seen their beautiful adobe home outside Taos on the rim of the Grand Canyon. They built this house themselves at ages 50 – 60, with little money and some help with the big poles and such from their kids. The house was far from finished, but very impressive, warm and artistically creative and beautiful.

.

Bryden was in fair shape, he could walk, although he had to drag one leg to do so. Driving was out. Bryden had a hard time talking, but he could be understood. Teri jumped right in and with multiple acupuncture treatments and body work daily, pulled Bryden back.

Day by day we saw improvement, and after a month he felt he was ready to drive his pickup to the main road into town, about a mile of dirt road from their house. I volunteered to go along to ride shotgun. I suggested that if he had to use the brake he just grab his pants at knee level, pick up his leg with his hand and arm and throw it at the pedal. The ride was okay, but at the juncture of the main road as I was about to take over driving, Bryden gunned the truck onto the main road into town. I wasn't sure that I was ready for that!

This dubious move went well enough, but Bryden hadn't had to use the brake yet either. Bryden turned off the road and again I thought he was ready to turn over the driving to me. Instead, he asked me if I wanted to see the floor of the Grand Canyon. BEFORE I COULD ANSWER, Bryden sped off on a switchback of a donkey trail, a terrifying 700-foot grade down to the canyon floor. What a ride! By the time we pulled up to the house later in the afternoon, I was still shaking.

I decided right then that Bryden could certainly manage without further help from us. Teri gave Joan acupuncture points to massage for Bryden's continued treatment and we flew back to heavenly Carriacou and our next boat. Or so we thought.

The island of Carriacou had stolen our hearts, and it felt very good to be back. Some of the people recognized us and welcomed us back as if we were natives. We loaded our five suitcases- everything we possessed in the way of "stuff" - into a combi and off we went to move aboard our new boat. Unfortunately, as with many ventures in life, this story had a twist of an ending.

The old Dane showed up as we stood there on the pier next to "our" boat with our luggage. "The deal is off", the Dane said, handing us our deposit. His partners in the boat didn't want to sell her he reported. That was the first we had heard of partners, and although shocked, disappointed and a little angry, we dragged our stuff down the long pier and checked into mosquito heaven, the Yacht Club. Escaping the blood suckers, at first light, we set about to find a place to rent. Teri went one way and I the other in our all-out search.

Teri, while following a lead, met up with another Dane, Tom, who owned a small complex on top of the hill above the boat yard and overlooked the entire bay. He was off to Denmark in a couple of days for at least a year and would rent us an A frame house with a kitchen down below. Tom's house was up a rise and just next door. He asked us to keep an eye on his house and offered his porch for us to use. The porch overlooked all of Tyrell Bay and its anchored cruising yachts and 180 degrees south over the reefs and on to Grenada in the distance all for the grand sum of $2400 for the entire year. We jumped at the chance and moved all the bags up a walking path to the top of the hill and Tom's place and moved in. His place was next to the spread owned by a local guy who had a flock of sheep and another of goats. The sheep were penned, but the 50 or so goats roamed around the top of that hill and our house at will. Never having lived around livestock, we learned a lot about goat behavior that year and never tired of watching the newly born kids scampering around, butting heads, and playing king of the rock within days of being born.

We loved living on top of that hill, with its breath-taking views of Tyrrell Bay and southward toward Grenada and all the small islands and reefs in-between. We'd sit watching the trade winds blow enormous thunderheads past our perch; their darkness contrasting ominously with the startling array of hues and shades, a symphony in blues and greens played out among the various reefs.

During that year we met just about every expat living on the island, there not being many, and most of the locals living in Tyrrell Bay. The peace and beauty of living there was in sharp contrast to the horror and shame of watching the U.S. conduct their Shock and Awe treatment of the people of Iraq on the one television on our part of the island. We stopped looking at television and stepped back in time.

Carriacou has no ground water. All fresh water is by catchment systems, water collected from the rains and channeled into holding tanks. Mosquito eating small minnows are given to each household by the local government to be placed in these catchment tanks to keep mosquito larvae from maturing. Almost all houses were built to store water in the lowest, coolest place below the house. The island was ablaze with flowers and tropical fruits as there was much rain, and when it rained, it poured.

Our house came with a circular green house. Open to the sun and rain, it was protected from the birds by mesh screening and a low block wall and entry door kept the animals out. We hadn't had a garden together before and set about developing one. We had good fertilizer at our door step, courtesy of the goats, protection from everything and lots of water, as Tom, the enterprising Dane, had built holding cisterns beneath every structure in his complex. We watched, thrilled, as the new shoots of our first plants appeared. We added more, filling the greenhouse. Then after a couple of months we noticed our first sick plant. We couldn't see why it was wilting so, but in a day it was on its side and I pulled it out. Where the roots should have been, there was a large ball of moving fire ants! We had already had a few encounters with ants in the house. Now we found them to be swarming under the soil, not only here in our garden, but, as it turned out, beneath the whole island. This was our first horrible encounter with the fire ants of Carriacou; we were to have many more. The ants made short work of all the roots in our garden. We had met the true rulers of paradise.

The wonderful outside shower with a startling view of the lovely harbor soon bit back, courtesy of the fire ants. After a refreshing shower one day I found myself afire. These resourceful critters had run up my towel, hanging from a nail in the wall. A billed cap I had put on when leaving the house on a walk down to the beach had harbored several of these devils that made their presence known in unison, and to the amusement of people gardening nearby, caused an extemporaneous dance by an obvious mad man hitting himself on his head, while jumping around! We found these bastards in our bed beneath our pillows one night. As beautiful as it was, Carriacou, or land surrounded by reefs, could just as well been named land held hostage by fire ants!

Many times a day, we'd gaze out our open windows and over the anchorage of Tyrell bay. We both longed to be there among our friends riding at anchor in one of the most picturesque spots in the Caribbean. We ramped up our efforts of finding our next boat. We asked our friends in Trinidad to look around for a cheap rental so we could really look there at all the yards and boat storage areas.

Already missing the constant cooling trade winds of Carriacou, we were back in the heat and mugginess of Chagaramas. Our friends, Jeff and Dawn had found us a place on an island near Chagaramas that required us to take a small wooden launch back and forth to the mainland. We could set up housekeeping there for the time we needed to find a boat. I've forgotten how much that modern cabin rented for, but I know it wasn't much, as nothing is very much in that economy. Lunches out at a café near the boat yards, frequented by all the crews working in them, featured the heavily flavored Indian cuisine and would cost about two dollars. Happy hours down on the waterfront restaurants were full of sailors and their crew members from the world over. It was a fantastic place to pick up all sorts of valuable information and great stories. We'd sweat out the previous night's excesses the following morning as we walked the boat yards looking for 'our' boat. The heat was beginning to take its toll, but a cold beer was always a few steps away in those yards.

It was in this heat that we found our next boat, a 37-foot sloop, *Sonador*- a seagoing, full-keel Marconi sloop.

The boat was well-built by the Canadian seller who lived on the island with his new wife. It was strong, well-equipped and very beautiful. Steve had used one log of mahogany to finish the interior, its matching grains and rich color created a cozy warm atmosphere. It had a very good layout for two; a small diesel and a self-steering vane. Steve built her in Canada and sailed her singlehanded to the Mediterranean and after many years there singlehanded her down the west coast of Africa and back across the Atlantic to Trinidad. *Sonador* was going for a song, so we jumped. I had heard for many years that Trinidad and Venezuela were great places to find a boat at bargain prices and it certainly was for us. Chagaramas has three or four large boat yards all of which allow owners to work on their own boats and there is much work going on, despite the merciless heat. The anchorage where we were and the people in the yards all monitored the morning marine VHF radio net. It was on the net that items were offered for free or trade. Bargains galore and just a great place to outfit or maintain your boat on the cheap. Trinidad offered us an economy we hadn't experienced, even cheaper than Mexico had once been.

We spent a short time outfitting the boat and waiting for US Coast Guard to send us our new documentation papers. These were necessary for us to enter any country. While waiting and acclimating to the rhythm and heat we experienced Mardi Gras Trinidad-style, with its steel drum bands and the most fabulous costumes. We had seen pictures and movies that featured this annual event, but being in the middle of it, not to mention the frantic pace of the weeks leading up to it, was a number one experience, totally surreal. We had a ball and met many locals and travelers who were in just for this event. We were invited to share a joint beside a rum shop with two natives who lived in New York City, but came back to their island for this event each year. One worked for the U.N., the other was a stock broker. They had gone to school together here on the island and had been returning for Mardi Gras for 15 years without missing one!

The bands all compete for the Best of Carnival prize, and sitting/standing on the truck bed or a bus frame on wheels, with 20 or so players and their steel drums ,defying gravity, somehow hanging on, and managing to play their parts. As the competition at Mardi Gras grew nearer, they would practice throughout the night. The costumes and costume makers are at it full time. They say as soon as Mardi Gras ends they get to work right away for next year's show. The days of the competition include maybe 50 bands from every town on the island and several from Port of Spain, the main city. Those trucks springs holding up the band would strain to breaking, the whole truck and all those on it, would be bouncing down the street as they played. Everything was rocking; it was fabulous! We did pay to sit in the grandstands, but all the action was happening in the fields beside the main stage and the grandstand area. This was the free, "people's area." It was in these adjacent fields that people set up their food and rum shops, just for the days of competition. Passing by, and practicing there until they were called to perform, were all the bands, each with their own music. Everyone was a movin' and a groovin', many scantily clad. The women of Trinidad, most a mix of Indian and African heritage, were the most beautiful either Teri or I had seen in one place, strikingly so.

We soon had our papers and cast off for Grenada to the north, beating into wind and seas coming straight at us, unimpeded from Africa. Trying our best not to get swept to the west and Panama was a very good test not only for the new boat but also her crew since we had been off the water for a while. All proved sound and after exploring The Spice Island we sailed to tiny Carriacou, part of Grenada, but, 25 miles north and a world away.

Chapter 8

Carriacou on Water

The northern Caribbean's hustle and bustle, with large charter fleets around the US and British Virgins and down to busy St. Maarten, makes Carriacou seem like heaven to those of us lucky enough to have spent time there. Carriacou consisted of three main villages, Hillsborough, Windward and Tyrrell Bay, each having its own distinctive style.

Hillsborough, on the western and leeward side, was the main town and contained 90%

of the island's commerce. There was one main road ringing the seafront, a couple of blocks either side of the main pier. The catamaran ferry arrived each day at this pier where the customs building also stood. Restaurants and services were available here, more or less.

The small hamlet of Windward, on the north coast, was exposed, although it sat behind a fringed reef, and offered a safe anchorage if you could find your way in. Walking the beach with its overhanging coconut palms and small residences fringed with flower gardens was always a treat and we never tired of it. We'd sit and chat with the old boat builders and marveled at their skill at making their efforts look easy. Windward has been a base for Scottish boat builders and fisherman for some two hundred years. Now the town consisted of many McLaughlin, MacTavish and Mc Andrews. The people here were light skinned.

Carriacou is located at 12 degrees north latitude, an imaginary line that the insurance boys deemed to be out of the hurricane zone. Our first chore was to find the hurricane hole, the safest place to anchor in case of a bad blow. We anchored our boat in the southwest corner of Tyrell Bay and set off by dinghy to explore the hidden corner to the north, a large tidal salt pond surrounded by mangroves. We found the narrow entrance to the mangroves, and mentally chose some spots that looked like the best places to ride out a storm, should such an emergency sanctuary ever become necessary.

Tyrrell bay consisted of a cluster of buildings along the waterfront road and beach, a couple of guest houses, a few restaurants, a market, a waterfront bar at the end of the cargo pier, a few rum shops scattered along the narrow beach road, and at the end, Jerry's boatyard.

Trading schooners were built on the island in the town of Windward only eight miles to the north as the crow flies. Windward, sitting behind a barrier reef, pushed the clock back a hundred years. Small clapboard New England style cottages with their shuttered windows overlooked the small neighboring island of Petit Martinique and the Grenadines to the north.

The seas surrounding this idyllic spot contained every shade of blue imaginable, so bright that it hurt to look at them for long.

Schooners up to 70-feet were built on the beach here with wood brought up from Guyana. The schooners were built super strong, but not to last forever, since the galvanized nails used in the construction would rust out over the next several years, but never mind, the schooners made enough to pay for themselves, in short order.

The schooners used the sole pier in Tyrrell bay. Cargo was loaded the same way it had been done since the first boat was built, by hand, with the aid of a block and tackle off a boom.

As for the cruising world, Jerry's boatyard was the center of all boat needs and boat storage for those who had to go back home for whatever reason, most hoping to schedule a return the coming season. Not too many people know about Carriacou, but its neighboring country and its islands, St. Vincent and the Grenadines, drew many charters from all over the world to spend a week or two in these waters of paradise.

Some charters ventured south to share our anchorages, but sailing between the islands could sometimes be quite rough with 12-foot seas and reinforced trades keeping boaters honest. Charter boats passing through would drop anchor in Tyrrell bay and row ashore for fun and meals.

A favorite haunt of theirs, and ours, was a beachfront open-air pizza place, run by two single Italian beauties, Daniela and Luciana. Daniela was going with Jerry, the English owner of the little boatyard.

Jerry was a very capable guy and was the area's "go to guy" for almost anything. Jerry was responsible for building a new commercial pier in the bay, replacing an old pier damaged in a storm. He had a fleet of seagoing tugs and barges. His crews hauled building materials, sand, gravel and the like throughout the islands.

Jerry chartered a private plane to search for three fishermen who had gone missing in a panga. He was credited with having the perseverance to continue the search for days until the fishermen and their boat were spotted many miles to the west and a rescue boat was sent out to fetch them.

Life on Carriacou was always a hoot. Rowing in, pulling the dink up on the beach and having drinks and sharing pizza with traveling sailors from around the world was so easy. Great stories and very colorful characters were the rule, not too many ex-pats, there being not much to do here. If you were self-contained, as most cruisers who traveled with their floating homes were, life was fantastic. Being able to see 30 feet down to the bottom where we were anchored watching turtles, rays, and many varieties of fish, was always entertaining. Falling into that water to have a float, on the shady side of the boat to cool off at midday, was heaven. All boats had shade awnings of some sort and as long as one kept the direct sun off the decks and cabin top, offered relief from the heat. The trade winds almost always blew, adding to that relief.

Sailing downwind to Grenada we were able to watch the Grenada Island Boat Races, a popular annual event which is held off of Gran Anse Beach in the south. What a ball! The captains had to make a running start from the beach to their boats, which were being held stern to the beach by one crewman. Three or four men would sail these wooden double-enders, called "two bows", with way too much sail up, around a several mile course and finish again at the beach. Wild!

The names were great too. I remember one named *Weapon of Mass Destruction*. The rum flowed. Another work boat regatta was held in Carriacou and one in Bequia to the north.

My son Colin was coming to Grenada to be with his girl friend from whom he had been separated for several months. Rose had been traveling the world on a school-sponsored program and was now visiting with her Californian parents who lived Grenada. We toured the island on the local mini vans while waiting for Colin to arrive. Although very beautiful, Grenada didn't draw us like Carriacou. There seemed to be an undercurrent of 'unwelcomeness' on the faces of the locals and it never felt as safe as our little island.

The reunion of us all was cause for

celebration that went on for some days. Taking Colin and Rose with us we set sail north for Carriacou so we could show off our new home. After an idyllic visit the love birds took flight and we were left to enjoy doing nothing at anchor.

Tyrrell bay was the largest anchorage around the island, and of course, had the hurricane hole as well. We, like others, used Carriacou as a base during the hurricane season and never ventured very far from that hole, at that time of year.

A fisherman friend of ours offered to take us out fishing with him. His boat, similar to the Mexican panga but of wood, was built there on the island. He fished, trolling for anything, but usually caught barracuda, which is what we helped him catch. His lines, one of which I was handling, was bailing wire! Pull it into your area of the boat and it attended to itself if that's what you could call it. It worked on the theory of last-in first-out, and worked flawlessly... a grand springy ball of wire tending to itself with little guidance from the fisherman.

Teri helped a local Englishman to quit smoking with the help of acupuncture and guided imagery. Word spread quickly. On an island of several thousand black folks, whenever one of the 50 or so white residents did anything out of the ordinary it warranted close attention. We used a portion of the beach in front of the rum shop/restaurant "Lambie Queen" to land and tied our dinghy to a palm tree there. Tables sat amongst towering palms and brilliant bougainvilleas and hibiscus, overlooking the beach beneath the palapa roof, very funky and a way low-key area.

One morning we were met by a Rasta who had seen better days. He smiled and asked Teri if she was the one who cured people of smoking. He loved his ganja but he wanted to quit cigarettes altogether. The next morning Teri arrived in the dinghy with her special ear needles, alcohol, cotton and tweezers to the enthusiastic reception of the local Rasta community. The bar owner and some hard-case, early morning drinkers were also huddled round for close inspection. With the bar owner's permission, Teri had this guy lie on the top of a couple of tables under the low palapa roof. Everyone now formed a tighter circle, all with loud exciting questions or comments, all wide-eyed, even the drunks, while Teri adjusted some needles in her newest patient's ear. It was quite a show.

There is a type of bootleg rum called "Jack Iron". Anyone sailing down around this part of the Caribbean knows it for its reputation, it's 151 proof, and will seriously imperil even the most seasoned veteran. I developed a fondness for it and imbibed it in addition to my daily wine intake. There was a local T-shirt depicting a skeleton with a hat, holding a bottle of Jack Iron while dancing his bones down the hill. So it was appropriate that I be wearing that very T-shirt when my heart STOPPED!

We had arrived at a secluded beach restaurant, owned by Coconut Joe and his Swedish wife. I had a puff or two on Joe's spliff, he being a Rasta. As he wandered away, I was sitting with Teri, and a rum and coke, on the porch, when I keeled over. Teri responded immediately. Finding no pulse, she went for the" Heart One" point in Chinese medicine. Located up in the center of your armpit, you can feel it for yourself:

Description of Heart 1 and its location in the armpit:

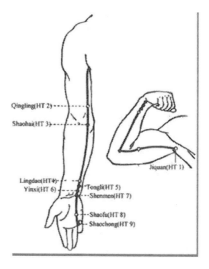

Chinese Name*: Jiquan (English translation: Supreme Spring)*

Location: *At the apex of the axillary fossa, where the axillary artery pulsates. In layman's terms, this point is found in the arm pit just under the front fold of the muscle. Using your finger to jam on this point, point your finger up towards the middle of the crest of the shoulder – as if you were trying to skewer up into the center of the armpit –*

where you will feel an ache deep in the muscles of the armpit.

Indications:

- *Chest congestion, shortness of breath, sad, anxious*
- *Apoplexy, hemiplegia, pain in the shoulder and arm, distention and pain in the chest and hypochondrium*

Functions: *Frees the chest, activates the meridian, and benefits the arm.*

Needling: *Perpendicular or oblique insertion .3 - .5 cun. Keep away from the axillary artery.*

Good thing to know! After a couple of minutes of Teri's massaging this *Heart One* point with great vigor, first on my left side and then on my right, I did come back. I had been in complete peace and from my perspective saw green fields rolling away with people wearing white with a bit of red, gathered in the far corner. They weren't clearly defined, as they were at a distance. A sound jarred me out of this calmness. I could hear Teri's voice shouting at me. I was very reluctant to leave this serene space but I came back. After gathering my wits and equilibrium, Teri and I walked up the steep hill, got into the next bus, and out to the last stop, where we fell into our dinghy, and returned to the *Sonador* at anchor. I stayed in the boat for 40 days, lost 40 pounds as well as most of my strength. Teri shone, giving me daily acupuncture treatments. She plied me with herbs and remedies sent to us by our friend Diana, a Medical Intuit from California. Eventually I could swim in the clear warm waters where we were anchored. Our friend Katherine rowed over daily to bring us fresh water, all contributing to my recovery.

This was summer, hurricane season, and

everyone monitored the weather closely since hurricane Earl was heading west along our latitude. By insurance standards, no such hurricane was meant to be. Old-timers in the anchorage were predicting it would turn north towards St. Lucia and Martinique, and pass us by. Others were already raising anchors and either heading south to the protection of some fjord-like bays on the south coast of Grenada, where they felt they'd be safer or, into the mangroves right here. We chose the mangroves because they were close; I hadn't gained my strength back, and was still skin and bone, and so the closer and more familiar, the better.

We were happy that we had already checked out the storm anchorage. With much effort we hauled our anchor for the first time in almost two months, only to find that our preferred spots had already been taken, so we fell back and dropped our main anchor, backed down, and made fast to the mangrove roots in our section of the outer, deeper pond. We were next to a large, rusting and badly dented, red cargo boat of violent character. On the other side was a newish 50-foot modern sloop. We put out our two other anchors with their chain and line, and set them 45° from the main anchor, a Delta-50 pounder with all the chain we had.

We did the same using our old inflatable dink, placing many lines from all points of our boat, to the roots of the amazing mangrove trees. The roots of these mangroves were covered with small, razor sharp oysters. Many scratches and slices later we set to removing everything from the deck including taking the main sail off the mast and boom, to reduce windage.

It turned out that our first hurricane Earl decided to make everyone wrong and started slanting south of us. Earl finally hit Grenada where many had gone to the safety of its fjords. Grenada got hit full on with 120 mph winds and yet 30 miles to the north in our little bay, we only got 100 miles an hour. Seventy-five percent of the roofs in Grenada were blown off, not just homes but government buildings as well. Once the roof of the jail was ripped off the prisoners were let out because the government couldn't care for them. Cruisers who were caught at anchor in the port of St Georges had chilling stories to tell. Prisoners riding in small boats threatened the small group of cruisers, waving their machetes, while prowling the anchorage. The sailors formed groups, armed with flare guns and shotguns to stand watches to protect their boats and crews day and night. The Grenada Coast Guard and police were nowhere in sight.

Our friends from Grenada arrived on the first ferry to Carriacou after the storm bringing empty suitcases to fill with food and staples to inconspicuously take back to Grenada and their home as looting had emptied all the unprotected and unguarded stores there.

When standing at the half open companionway, bobbing and holding on, we could see out through the spindrift to thirty or so other boats doing the same as we; looking at the wonder of our hurricane. The surges rocked the boat, but the wind was at our stern and our lines and spring lines to the roots were holding and not chafing. We listened to the radio with interest and relief when we learned that we would be spared the worst.

The mangroves were a great buffer and we were really deep in them, still the noise of a great storm like this one was frightening and kept us in a constant state of tension. People who thought they had taken great precautions in ridding their decks and spars of anything not part of the boat itself, found surprises as things came loose and simply took flight. Spindrift and a mix of mangrove leaves and foam constantly flew by our boat.

After several hours of intense winds, that hurricane finally passed and things slowly went back to normal. We were worn out by all the preparations and chose to stay put for a couple of days as we watched others leave the mangroves and return to their favorite anchorages. After a few days we pulled all our anchors and went back to our area of Tyrrell bay to settle in.

A couple of weeks later we repeated this

survival exercise but this time we knew exactly where we wanted to be and gave ourselves more time to prepare. This time I decided to run, bow first, into the mangroves. We let the anchor go a hundred and fifty feet from the edge of the trees, and ran over the chain as it ran out quickly. The bow was secured to the mangroves, and from the stern we set our other anchors out at angles from our main anchor. Now secured, we were ready for bigger Ivan.

We waited three days in the quiet of the mangroves, watching boats arrive - charter boats, mono hulls and big cats. The catamarans could make it over the bottom at the shallow, narrow entrance to the main pond, which was large enough to hold anyone capable of entering its shallow entrance. So the cats went inside with some smaller sail and power boats. We, who drew almost seven feet, had to be where we were this time, in the smaller, outer and deeper part of the mangroves. This is where we had been weeks earlier, again among the large cargo schooners and other rough-looking rusty steel cargo boats.

The wind hit our bow which was secured to the mangrove roots. With the companionway facing aft and after from the wind force, the door was free to be open, allowing us to experience the storm up close. The rain and blizzard of mangrove leaves flew over and around us. Below decks, we stayed dry but hot, taking it all in. We had neighbors on either side of us. At some point a large 80-foot dark-hulled cargo schooner came dragging down quickly through our pond. Its anchor was pulling up all the stern anchors of our neighbors. The schooner passed just feet off our stern, and somehow left us unscathed, but not without trouble.

While still daylight we watched in fascination as a big canvased jib came loose on a schooner moored to a barge across from us. This smaller sail, normally bound to its front position, flapped itself to shreds, emitting sounds like gunshots. The schooner broke free of her bow lines, but still secured by her stern, turned 180 degrees and held there through the storm.

When the storm had passed, early the next morning, we ventured out on deck, there to see six inches of solid mangrove leaves covering the decks!

Our anchors held but others' did not; consequently, we found four boats leaning against *Sonador*. Our neighbors, much like Huey, Dewey, and Louie, plus one, were pressed against one another all at the same angle and the whole lot had pulled down on us. Those four boats pushed against our one large, round industrial-strength fender now compressed to a six inch pancake against our hull. If that thing had popped under the pressure, it would have been heard clear down in Grenada.

Back to back hurricanes wore me out and we decided to go back to the States for some medical checks. It had been a hellish month since my heart had stopped.

When the doctor returned to Carriacou from a month's absence I saw him, a Cuban who chose to stay after the U.S. invasion of Grenada a few years prior. He hooked me up to the only EKG machine on the island and confirmed Teri's suspicions that I had had a heart event in the month before.

We reserved a spot on the Dockwise yacht transporter that was leaving Martinique – three islands north of ours - in a few weeks for the Miami /Fort Lauderdale area. So despite Teri's deep concern for my stamina after such a heart event in the middle of nowhere we sailed up to the land of supermarkets, cheeses and croissants, treating ourselves to all things French. For the first time in my life I needed to put weight on, what a pleasure.

The trip north took us to Bequia, St. Vincent, the Grenadines, and a favorite of ours St. Lucia, and the fabulous Tetons where we anchored for a rest. We spent a day at a hole-in-the-wall anchorage where it turned out *Pirates of the Caribbean* was filmed. We recognized several sites that appeared in the movie.

Once anchored in Martinique we toured the island while awaiting the arrival of Sonador's ride. The day of loading arrived. Guided by directions delivered by loudspeaker, we motored into the incredible yacht transport boat and secured ourselves to the inside walls of this ship, aided by the crew. The ship is really a self- propelled dry dock. The transom is dropped and the whole ship sinks down 15 feet or so to allow yachts to power in and park. When loaded, the transom is raised into sea going position; water is pumped out and the yachts are in place, fully supported with bracing put in place by divers and ready to travel to their destination. We found it to be a great service.

We bid our *Sonador*, adieu, till Ft. Lauderdale. We met her a month later and sailed her up to Stuart, a familiar place for us. Then we had her hauled out and loaded onto a yacht transporter. Although it was Christmas time and snowing in the Rockies, we found a guy who would truck her across the U.S. to San Francisco, California.

Carriacou is a wonder, a very beautiful, friendly, safe and quiet small island. We loved our time there, but after a while, despite all that beauty, the desire for a little something more arises and that's what happened to us. The heart event sealed it for us and we were looking forward to being closer to the kids and grandson and seeing old friends and places again. All we had to do was find a berth for *Sonador* in Sausalito that would allow us to live aboard, no longer an easy thing to do.

Chapter 9

Boquete and Bocas del Toro, Panama

Our luck held and we got the last available live aboard berth in all of Sausalito. Although it cost a small fortune getting the boat there, living aboard for only berth rent, would pay for itself in short order. I'm an ex-Marine, so it was off to the Veterans Hospital for a check of my heart. With the second EKG in a few months' time and with all the other medical testing they had available, they could find no reason for continued concern. Yes, they could see that there had been an episode, but now all looked ok. No medication recommended. What a relief!

With no health reasons to keep us in the States and after being in town for only nine months, we took out an ad in our favorite sailing magazine, *Latitude 38*, and sold the *Sonador* to the first caller. The boat, by Northern California standards, was a great deal for the buyer, a female cop. Since we had bought it at such a bargain price in Trinidad we could let her go at a good price and still cover all costs associated with bringing her here to the West Coast. So, without our home, in the land of high rents, we got the map out once again. Where now?

When in Carriacou, we had read and heard of the experiences of fellow cruisers who were heading west from the Eastern Caribbean, and having reached Panama, had taken some time to explore. The stories that most impressed us were accounts of finding a cooler paradise at 4000 feet elevation in the north of Panama. At sea level, being so close to the equator, the climate was too hot to bear.

Nestled in the mountains of Chiriquí and on the flanks of the dormant volcano, *Volcan Baru,* sits the charming village of Boquete, close to the border with Costa Rica. This was the paradise travelers hailed. At that elevation, Boquete boasted spring -like weather year round - a haven of cascading streams, a pageant of flowers and coffee farms.

Boquete was rapidly becoming a popular retirement or second home destination, mainly for Americans and Canadians with some Europeans as well. Living there was cheap, especially after Marin County, and the quality of life index very high. It was appealing enough to cause a land boom there. People were scrambling to put their money down on something while spending every waking hour touring the area to find what suited them best.

Panama welcomed people with retirement income, and only required a couple to show an income of $600 a month to qualify as *Jubilados* (Spanish for *retired person*). We learned that such status entitled the couple to large discounts on all things from airline tickets and meals to busses and movies. Some of the discounts were as high as twenty-five percent, as was the case with airline tickets.

Jubilados didn't need to leave the country every six months as one would be required to do on a simple vacationer's visa. *Jubilados* were allowed the luxury of multiple entries and exits. Medical care at hospitals in both

Panama City and David (just an hour's drive down the mountain from Boquete) was first rate. The best part was it was fraction of the cost in the States.

We had always been salt-water dependent so we figured with Panama's two coastlines one on the Caribbean, and one on the Pacific; we would be able to find something appealing. We also knew how fast we were capable of burning through the money received from the sale of the *Sonador* and that we'd better find an investment for that money sooner rather than later.

So off we flew once again, looking for our own version of paradise. Our requirements were: safe, beautiful, friendly; affordable, stable of government, offering modern health care and welcoming to foreigners. Boquete seemed to fill the bill.

The long dormant Volcano *Baru* sounded a

bit ominous, but on the other hand, offered spectacular views. Farming was carried out on the flanks of the volcano, offering an artist's pallet, a patchwork of colorful crops stitched together up its slopes. The weather was, as reported, almost a constant seventy degrees, year round. A half- million acre National Forest was shared with neighboring Costa Rica. Hikers setting off from Boquete enjoyed pristine surroundings in all directions. Roaring, cascading streams and world-class rapid runs on the bigger rivers drew people from the world over, and supported many outdoor guides and eco tour companies.

We found a very nice three bedroom home with a wrap-around veranda and views down the length of the valley and over to the Volcano. The clouds would blow over the mountains from their source on the Caribbean side, causing rainbows to arc over the valley on a daily basis. We met and became fast friends with our neighbors, Mikey and Hershel who had built their home, and had been living in it for 3 years. Hershel was an ex-pat community leader and had helped start the weekly Gringo meetings that was held in English at the oldest and most popular hotel in town, The Panamonte. Some 50 to 70 people would show up for these weekly gatherings, where guest speakers would talk about things of interest to investors, builders, renters, and retirees settling in a new and very different country. These gatherings were an ideal place to meet your neighbors and find answers for many of the questions shared by all. The subject most gringos were interested in was real estate, and this land-rush created a feverish atmosphere, a sort of feeding frenzy, something we had never experienced before or since.

Real estate companies lined the main street. You couldn't meet any American without being asked if you had found your land yet. This, of course, was our intention and the first thing we did was to find and buy a car that would allow us to go anywhere so we could familiarize ourselves with what was available. We settled on a used Japanese Jeep-like vehicle with four-wheel drive and a five-speed diesel engine. We felt we'd be better off exploring on our own, rather than talking to the real estate people, who we viewed as sharks. We spoke and understood Spanish, more or less, and could read a map, so each day would find us exploring a new area, circling further each day from the center of Boquete. We would follow trails to their end, talking to the locals as we went. They were very friendly, welcoming and helpful.

We learned something that few gringos there knew, that there was a proposed road, to connect Boquete with the large farming community on the other side of Volcan Baru.

This road would span grand scale chasms, traverse forest and jungle, and cross countless streams and creeks. We talked to the road crews at the end of the line and got some idea of when this undertaking would be completed. We did an end run around to the other side of the mountain, and worked our way back toward Boquete in our search.

We got lucky and met a man who had to sell his property. He had a seven acre coffee farm that was no longer functioning. The property was breathtakingly beautiful. A walk through it revealed a small creek on either side and while walking all the way through the jungle of trees, ancient ferns and impatiens of pink, magenta and white, we were visited by the huge, fairy-like Blue Morpho butterflies. Those occasional flashes of iridescent blue let us know this was a special, magical place.

It turned out that the property owner's son

had been driving when he had an accident, killing the other driver. The car belonged to the father, and was uninsured. This put our new friend in a bad spot. To keep his son out of prison, he had to sell everything in his name and do so before the end of the year. The pressure was on. His asking price, although low to begin with, continued to drop each time we met with him. We finally agreed and bought the land for a fiftieth of what raw land in Boquete was selling for in those gold-rush days. The best part was that the farm would be a stone's throw from the new connecting road when it was completed. We found an English-speaking attorney in our nearby city of David and legalized the deal with her.

We had been living in Boquete for three months and had taken care of business. Now that we had hopefully invested wisely, and hadn't burned through the *Sonador's* proceeds, we were free to live within our means and continue to explore new possibilities. Our new budget demanded that we find more economical housing, so we settled on a two bedroom cottage, several minutes' drive from town center. With the savings on rent, this one costing $400 a month, we were able to spend time on the Caribbean side of Panama, the Bocas Del Toro area, while keeping our base in the highlands.

The main town of Bocas Del Toro was on the biggest of the island group, a destination of many of our fellow cruisers and had been talked and written about extensively over the past few years. We loved being back on the blue-green waters and after finding our own boatman, Bacho, set out to explore this very primitive and pristine area.

One of the many islands, Bastimentos, hosted many international surfing competitions and was a magnet for hippie travelers on the Mayan Trail. The main town of Bocas was a boom town reminiscent of early Key West with a bit of Deadwood thrown in. The funkiness of the place won our hearts immediately but the heat was oppressive. Although on the same latitude as Carriacou, Bocas was shielded from the Caribbean's cooling trade winds by other islands that surrounded it, leaving it hot, moist and still. As nice and appealing as it was to us in so many ways, the heat was a factor we had no solution for. A long time friend of Teri's had bought land nearby to Bocas Town, on the same greater body of water but on another island. We asked Bacho to take us there so we could see what was appealing enough to draw her and her investments. She and her ex-husband, still close friends, bought land on the mainland side of the inland sea that includes Bocas. They also bought land a short boat ride away on a nearby island. The mainland property consisted of a100 acre cacao farm. Rising from water's edge straight up a steep hillside, in a jungle atmosphere, is where they grew their crop. It was a beautiful place, very primitive, with a local Indian family living there as workers and caretakers. They envisioned an organic approach, which would take a few years of work to achieve. The ex husband was in his paradise, and Teri's friend was free to return to her Texas base, whenever she wanted. We considered the possibility of living there on a boat, but in the end, that side was just too hot for us.

Back up in Boquete we started taking short one and two day trips to the Pacific side only an hour's drive away. We spent many enjoyable days and nights as guests of Mikey and Hershel in their new beach house down the coast, a couple of hours drive. Acting like true pioneers, they carved out a section of beach and built their second Panamanian house. Brave souls!

On the Pacific side as well, we were hammered by the heat and the mosquitoes. Something in each of us had been changing regarding our tropical heat tolerance; it was dropping. For years, summers in Mexico were tolerable, but Panama's coasts, while heaven for lovers of heat, sun, and beaches, were no longer possible for us. We were learning about our limits and the limits of latitudes in our continued search for that perfect place.

Boquete was a sweet spot to live in and if we had been content to be away from salt water, it would have suited us very well. The English-speaking group that formed our social contacts was mainly ex-pats. It was large enough with quite an interesting mix and more than a few kindred spirits. The town was a center for the coffee trade: growing, buying, roasting and exporting. The workers on the coffee plantations were indigenous and colorfully-clothed Guaymi Indians from an inaccessible jungle area on the eastern slopes of the volcano.

The Guaymis would move the whole family into the housing provided them by their employers: primitive brick hovels without doors or windows just breaks in the wall, right in the coffee fields. There they would work for the harvest time, about half a year, then move back to their villages deep in the bush. The women were all clothed in their particular tribe's colors and patterns with the kids in tow, youngsters of six carrying a sibling behind mom who would have the baby wrapped and slung in a shawl on her back.

The men only showed up in town on Saturday nights and were often seen still blind drunk on Sunday morning. Harvesting coffee is very hard work. The steep angles of some of the slopes would challenge a mountain goat! Coffee bushes with their distinctive leaves and berries, from green to bright red also contain little coffee bugs. They fly, and, like no-see-ums, are small but fierce. Working with them flying around and biting you would drive you mad; though these families carried on.

There were a few charities and organizations caring for these workers and their families, especially the children. We'd pass by their housing on our daily drive up high into the hills above Boquete. Often we would wave the kids over to our car to pass out clothes and food stuffs – it was like seeing children hailing from another era and a world of poverty.

I suffered an emergency as my belly swelled and tightened with unbearable pain. We rushed over to our local doctor. His quick diagnosis was that my appendix was about to burst.

He told us that he'd meet us at the hospital in David, an hour's drive away. We luckily had joined the hospital's health program, similar to insurance. As soon as we arrived I was admitted, prepped, and taken into the operating room. What speedy service. This proved to be a messy operation due to gangrene present in the appendix. The surgery was a success and the care at the hospital, warm, caring and personal was a pleasure to experience. After a few days I was able to convalesce at home. Although we had a few hundred dollars co-pay, the bill was mostly covered by our hospital's health plan. Had we had to pay ourselves, it still would have been a fifth of what it would have cost in California.

I recovered quickly, and we passed the days driving around the higher elevations among the various rapid running streams and drinking in the beauty of it all.

We expanded our guerilla-style of gardening. We would take shears with us and clip a piece of any plant that looked good. We would take it home and plant it in the ground then sit back and watch it grow. The place was so fertile that even fence posts would sprout. One of our favorite flowers was the datura, or deadly night shade plant. A large bell shaped flower that gave the most intoxicating fragrance. We had several take root, the flowers gave us immense pleasure in watching them grow. Living was good and very inexpensive; a three-part lunch in a local house or restaurant cost a few dollars, dinner was a couple of dollars more.

We decided to put together a top quality web site, and put the land out for sale. We'd had it for more than a year and all we'd done to it was have some paths cut through to facilitate the showing of the land to prospective buyers. We placed a healthy price on it, and the photos of the land showed well on the web site. We learned what was necessary to have your site come up among the top in several search engines, and we kept working at it.

We sold it when the buyer overheard us talking about it while he sat at an adjacent table in David's new *TGI Friday's* restaurant one afternoon. He was almost too good to be true and wanted to see it immediately. The deal went through smoothly, despite a little machismo on the part of his lawyer towards our lady champion. We had made a small fortune, being in the right place at not quite the right time, but close enough to cash in on the boom. Here again, like selling the bakery in Mexico, we ended up finding the buyer right under our noses. What a happy conclusion to a year and a half of land investing and selling. We were missing the sea, so despite the beauty, we said our goodbyes and went off in our continuing search for that special place. But where to next?

While in Carriacou, Jerry, the boat yard owner, had often spoken about the Azores, and what a fantastic place they were. He was planning to move there one day. Land and old houses were cheap there. The Island's views and settings looked fantastic and reports were that the people were very friendly. It all sounded good to us and would be an ideal place for a sailor to put down roots. Perhaps, we thought, we could parlay our winnings there. We read a piece, again in our favorite sailing magazine, *Latitude 38*, written by a professional sailing couple, raving about the Azores and the land deals available there. We were ready for a grand tour which would include checking out those islands, sitting in the middle of the Atlantic ocean. After a visit to the San Francisco Bay Area to see the kids and grandkids, it was off to Europe, visiting old friends and newer ones we met while cruising the Caribbean. We had great fun, living large along the way, but certainly didn't find our next place while over in Europe.

Completely oblivious to the start of summer vacation and the hordes that would be unleashed; we flew down to Portugal, the historic landlords of the Azores, in search of a ride out to those islands. It was a bad time for that, as everything had been booked for weeks. It turned out that while many Azorean men live and work abroad, they do come back at this time each year, bringing gifts and visiting the homestead.

We were sitting in a restaurant in Lisbon that specialized in big grilled meats Argentinean-style when we fell into conversations with some English speaking Portuguese travelers who were singing the praises of an island off the southern coast of Brazil, Santa Catarina, or as most called it, *Florianopolis* - the name of the island's main town. These were international travelers, some of them seasoned surfers, all of whom loved the place. They told us of its beauty, sensible pace, and freedom from crime. That last bit caught our attention, because we had always thought that, although beautiful, Brazil was a country with a very high crime rate. They told us that although 40 miles long, Santa Catarina connected to the mainland at only one point where its shore was within a couple of miles of the mainland, and that there was a bridge connecting the two at that point.

That one bridge saved the place since criminals stayed away from a place where there is only one road in and out. In addition to its lack of crime, there was a village located on the southern end of the island designated as a World Heritage site, as it had been colonized by Portuguese whalers in the 1700's. Some of the hamlets in the southern part of the island were said to be untouched by the passage of time. The more we heard, the more we were inclined to check out this supposed paradise in more detail. We love those laid-back beach locations – areas that time seems to have forgotten like Carriacou and Bocas Del Toro.

We came to our senses and put the Azores on the back burner. We've learned as most have, not to try to force things when they're not happening. We've learned to let go and move on to the next step.

So after some time in an internet café, we booked our flight to Rio and on to Florianopolis.

Our long transatlantic flight which went first

to Madrid then on to Rio, was a horrible one. Two unhappy infants kept us awake for the full 12 hours. We arrived at the Rio Airport at midnight exhausted and when passing through Immigration, were pulled aside and informed that since we didn't have any visas, we were to re-board that same plane and be returned to Madrid immediately!

The shock almost left Teri in a crying heap on the airport floor! Apparently because our country was making it more and more difficult for citizens of Brazil to enter the U.S., we American tourists were being given a pay back- a political tit for tat and there we were in the middle. Having had so much time and training in Mexico, I first tried to find a way around this bother, with a little consideration, shall we say. Sadly, that didn't fly.

There was one other flight preparing to leave,

this one to Buenos Aires, so I pleaded to be allowed to leave Brazil on that one. Since the travel agent in Lisbon had been incorrectly informed that no visa was necessary, the airline personnel there in Rio pleaded on our behalf and off we went to the Argentine capitol. We collapsed on that relatively short flight and were still groggy in the cab when we arrived at dawn into the downtown section of Buenos Aires, searching for a hotel.

After regaining our balance the next day, we set to explore the fabulous city of Buenos Aires and to locate the Brazilian embassy where we made our proper application for a six month visa. That process required our passports to be handed over while our application was being processed. During the week that we waited, we were free to sample the cosmopolitan good life in a new grand city, with its tangos and steaks, along with some tasty inexpensive local red wines.

Because of a recent devaluation of the currency in Argentina, all prices seemed cheap, especially compared with the European prices we had just experienced. Wide boulevards, old architecture, friendly people, and an economy that made the dollar stretch. We liked it and promised ourselves a return trip to explore the wine country and the Alpine area of Baraloche near the border with Chile, sometime soon. But for now, with a six month visa and the surfer stories still fresh, we couldn't wait to fly directly to Santa Caterina Island.

Chapter 10

Florianopolis, Brazil

Florianopolis, a modern skyscraper-filled, bustling city, sat half on the mainland and half on the island, divided by an inland sea, an unusual arrangement.

Once we landed, we entered into a more easy-going atmosphere, more relaxed than any we had found in Europe. Lots of Argentines came north to vacation in the developed northern half of the island. Rock stars from all over vacationed here with other beautiful people. This had made it a place to be seen during the season. International surfing championships were held off the many beaches along the east coast, facing huge waves coming in from the deep blue South Atlantic Ocean. Santa Catarina boasted 40 pure white sand beauties, all surrounded by the sub–tropical flora and fauna associated with these latitudes.

We were drawn to the pristine, undeveloped Heritage sites in the south of the island. Located there were the small Azorean-like villages that we had heard about - settlements that hadn't changed much in 300 years. In these few villages lived the direct descendants of the original Portuguese whalers who first settled there, some live in the original houses. Whaling had continued right up to recent times but now those whalers chose other fisheries to pursue.

A popular alternative fishery was the growing of oysters in nets that hung from wooden frames in the protected shallow waters of our west coast area, facing the high mountains of the mainland. The little community of Caiera, located on that protected western side, almost at the southern tip, was a World Heritage site, and pretty as a picture. Pastel colored cottages, with thick walls and shuttered windows with planters overflowing with flowers, side by side on narrow, cobblestone streets. Those on the water had small boat houses attached with ramps sloping down to the water. We had only seen such historical maritime history in the history books. Living here was like living in a museum. It was easy to see why they called this place the Tenth Azorean Island.

We were out one day looking for a small boat

yard we had heard was nearby. Upon finding it, we met its owner, Luis, and heard his amazing story. An Italian, Luis had trained as a violin maker in his parents' native land, but back in Brazil, Luis had turned his attention to the building of new speed boats. He and his crew of a few local apprentices were turning out boats designed in the style of Garwood, Chris Craft and other classics from the 30's and 40's. His clients were the very rich of Sao Paolo, to the north.

Luis and his family, including his elderly parents, sister and brother had cleared land for the boat yard. Across the only road and on the water, they carved out their compound. There they built a cluster of houses for themselves around on old stone mill built by the original settlers and certified a national historical site that could not be altered. The mill apparatus was a real museum piece, sporting wooden gears to run the great stone mills that were put into motion by a horse or bull going round in a circle. These days the mill house had become a gathering spot for family and friends who ate and drank among the Spirits who were obviously present there beneath those 300 year old hand-hewn beams.

We were offered Luis' sister's house to rent, as she was living in Paris. Her cabin was a small one bedroom, heated by a wood stove, on stilts, with no insulation in the walls. It was tucked in the trees at the edge of a small stream. It suited us perfectly. Peaceful, quaint, and natural, it afforded views of the bay through the trees and flowering bushes, a bit of heaven for $400 a month.

We were introduced to an English- speaking neighbor, a retired teacher who agreed to teach us Portuguese. After dealing with Spanish for many years, we thought

Portuguese was doable, but we were wrong. We found it to be impossible to try to get by on our Spanish. We still met the locals, and with our geeky Portuguese and some Spanish and English, would usually get the gist of whatever was being discussed but no more. Back in Mexico we referred to this form of communication as "Smile and Nod".

Our days revolved around lunch at a favorite restaurant, trying some new dining experience or exploring a new locale. We sought out the owners of our favorites, and often a nice friendship would ensue.

We needed a car and wanted to investigate immigration possibilities with a lawyer. One was recommended by the two professional women we had shared a couple of bottles of wine with, while fogged in at a small airport waiting for the connection between Buenos Aires and Florianopolis. We looked him up at their suggestion and we liked this guy especially since his English was very good. We had found a used car at a dealer, but weren't allowed to finalize the deal because we didn't have a national ID number. The lawyer helped us get one in an hour, following a visit to the right office. Ditto with opening a bank account, something we had had difficulty with in Grenada, Mexico and Panama. We asked the lawyer about the immigration possibilities. We hoped, like Panama, it wouldn't be too difficult. We already had copies of all the papers we needed to receive our Panamanian *Jubilados* visa. The lawyer assured us we would qualify and to simply leave it to him.

We can only guess, but we think that once he learned of our financial state, which was nothing to warrant his serious interest, he seemed to lose interest. Perhaps he was after bigger fish. The fine and expensive wines we had shared with his two women friends who had recommend him to us may well have given the mistaken impression that we were financial heavyweights. Yes, we were interested in land, and had discussed our interest with them, but 40K, not four million. In the end, the lawyer didn't come through for us in the way he had promised. Our immigration was not taken care of.

We lived on Santa Caterina Island for six months, had bought a car, an antique whale boat, some furniture, and had made a deposit on a waterfront fisherman's cabin with a boat house and small pier, just a short walk from the boatyard. All this we thought we were returning to as soon as the residency visa was granted to us back in San Francisco. That was the requirement: that you make your application from your home town. So the Brazilian Consulate in San Francisco was the place we had to travel to. The way the Immigration Officer in Brazil explained it to us, we thought that it would only require a short round trip and we'd be back in place, settling into Brazil. We knew we could stay with a friend in San Francisco, visit the family and be in and out in a couple of weeks. So we continued on, living the life near our south end of the island until our six month visa expired.

Always looking for a boat, whenever we are without one, just a few months before we had to leave we found a beauty in a fisherman's village, a couple of miles south of us. An authentic double ended whale boat, about 26-feet long. Built of local woods and of traditional lap strake construction, she was a rare find. Powered by a small one cylinder hand crank diesel engine, she was steered with a long tiller attached to an outboard rudder.

The boat had neither mast nor sail, but was equipped with rowing stations for a few stout men. This is what was used to hunt, kill, and then tow the dead whale back to the village for slaughtering.

We hired Luis to set a mooring for us behind the boat yard. We went into Florianopolis and met a friend of his who gave us a large old bus tire. His crew filled the tire with re-bar and cement and cured it for several days. Some local boys rolled it out on a minus tide to a spot where they were up to their necks in water. There they let it fall, right side up and we had our new mooring.

We found a sail maker and ordered a sprit sail along the original design of what was used in the time before motors. Luis would supply the spars. We visited a restaurant in another fishing village on the windward side, just over the hill from Caiera. The owner, a fisherman himself, first offered us a glass of cachaca the local aperitif, similar to homemade vodka, and then guided us through his restaurant, full of lively guests, to see his stable of fishing boats. All locally built, as ours, these were all working fishing boats which up until recently, were used to harpoon whales. There among the boats, in a large boat house on the beach, along with assorted spars, ropes, nets and buoys, sat some of the saltier residents, all whom we enjoyed a drink with, then another, even when we were reduced to sign language. They didn't care, they got a hoot out of these older gringos, ex-fisherman, owning one of their own craft and treated us like old friends and kindred spirits. The same scene would be repeated each time we arrived at his restaurant. We developed similar relationships with other locals, mainly the restaurant owners we were getting lots of exposure to. The fact that we were happy to share our dessert recipes, and work with their cooks to turn out the best desserts seen locally, put us in good stead with them and many meals and drinks came our way as honored guests.

One friendship was with an oyster grower we passed almost every day to and from town. He would get into his canoe and standing, pole out to his oyster rack hung with net cages full of oysters. There he'd hand pick a dozen of his best – pole back to the beach, put them on the floor and pressure wash them. Then he would shuck them, squeeze fresh lime on them and hand them to us. A dozen fresh from the sea, all this for the grand sum of two dollars. Needless to say, we saw much of our oyster man and his simple yet elegant life style.

There was another oyster farmer nearby, one with a larger operation. He had a large wooden building and boat house just across the street from our rental at the "Italian compound". He processed oysters there for wholesale, by the sack. Just next door to his operation and along the water's edge, stood several fishermen's shacks and some cottages that had been remodeled and rebuilt. Some had short wooden piers leading out to deeper water, and others had boat houses with ramps leading down to the water, in between. The shack closest to the oyster man was an old, one story cabin consisting of two rooms and a bath. It was a sparse and primitive, but livable, with lots of potential, seeing as it had 70 feet on the beach, and a pier and ramp for its adjacent boat house. A small yard, between it and the road, had several flowering and fruiting trees. The owner wanted $40,000 U.S. for it. After shopping around and looking at other places we came back to this one. We gave the guy a deposit to take it off the market, until we received our residency visa. He had had the property on the market, i.e. a small sign overgrown by a hedge, with a phone number and small lettering stating it was in fact for sale. Ours was the first interest in his property in over two years, so we didn't think that his taking it off the market for a couple of months would be a problem.

We spent time in the middle of the island, in the little town of Barra da Lagoa, to see the fishing boats come in with their catch of what was called "mullet", but this was a different fish than the mullet of the northern hemisphere. These were beautiful fish, averaging ten pounds in size, nice flaky, white meat fish. The fishermen would gill net them and fill their small boats, to the verge of sinking. We'd watch from a suspension walking bridge as they raced in the cut just a few meters beneath our feet to the protection of the inner harbor. As they passed beneath us we'd see all hands bailing for all they were worth mere inches to spare between a successful trip and a complete disaster. All in all, this was an amazing show. We watched, from a bluff, while local clubs manned the double-ended whale boats, and with three men to a side plus the helmsman standing in the stern, they would row their nets around in a circle to catch the school in a purse seine. Wonderful to witness - - this show - - how it had been done for hundreds of years, same place, same boats, same fish, and same men.

Surfers, board sailors and kite surfers from around the world gave the middle of the island, around the town of Lagoa, a very international and cosmopolitan flavor. Inviting sidewalk cafés in this small tourist destination were similar to many in the Mediterranean. We saw few fatties here; mostly young, tanned, athletic hard bodies.

One of our favorite dining experiences was the Churrascaria type. These were restaurants that featured meats of all kinds. Meats grilled on an open flame, served dramatically on a long spit carried high were the specialty here. Your table would have a green flag and a red one. If your green flag was flying, a server could pass by with a large cut of meat on a platter, prime rib, steaks, a skewer stacked with chicken hearts or melt-in-your-mouth pork cuts. They would offer to slice as many pieces as you wanted, until you said enough. Other servers would pass by, seeing your green flag and offer their specialty. The accompanying buffet table of all you could eat sushi, pastas, soups and salads were all washed down with the free cachaca moonshine. Once your plate was filled, you raised the red flag. This process would last for hours or until you burst. This style, sort of like revolving Dim Sum carts, had its origins in Argentina and the Pampas. This was Gaucho style. Our friend, Luis, had told us that this southern part of Brazil, felt more connected to the Gaucho cowboy tradition of their neighbors to the south - Paraguay, Uruguay and Argentina - than what one typically finds in the north, in Rio, and along the northern beaches of Bahia. Here in the southern most states, there were many Italians and Germans as well. In Blumenthal, the capitol of our state of Santa Caterina, one heard German spoken on the streets and in the shops. Blumenthal had a German language newspaper and Tyrollean architecture, with restaurants serving German food.

As our tourist visas were about to expire, we had a final meeting with our attorney and an official who, for a few hundred dollars, was going to arrange to have "our application placed on top of the pile in the Consulate in San Francisco, thus greasing the skids for us". Or so we were promised.

Teri's lifelong friend, Barbara, who was traveling for a month, offered us her house in San Francisco. It was a mansion compared to what we had been living in and only a half a block from Golden Gate Park. Clement Street with all the ethnic restaurants you could possibly imagine was just a short walk away. We were in foodie heaven: Chinese live fish markets, with live turtles bound and lying on their backs on the edge of the sidewalk, exotic fruits and vegetables. Asian, Italian, Indian restaurants, even Burmese, all our favorites were there. The Museums, first run movies, all within a half hour walk, kept us busy, but the reason we were up there was to get this visa.

We applied to the Brazilian Consulate, handing over original and notarized documents. Although we thought we'd been through all this with the Panamanian Government, Brazil had some real nit picking requirements that made it very difficult. For instance, our marriage certificate, from Mexico, where we had done the deed, needed to be officially stamped, by three levels of the Mexican government – city, state and federal. This could only be done by hand carrying the document to these different authorities, each of which was located in a different city. We hired the sister of a close Mexican friend to do the hand carrying for us.

Another time-consuming step in our making our application for residency was that our birth certificates had to be authenticated by the Brazilian Consulate nearest 'our place of birth'. For me that meant New York and for Teri Los Angeles. The notary's stamp and license needed to be authenticated and then returned to the San Francisco office of the Brazilian Consulate. On each visit more time consuming requirements were added. Nowhere were there any signs whatever that our 'skid greasing' had had an effect.

After weeks of waiting and document gathering for the Brazilians we were close to overstaying our friend's hospitality. Not sure what to do with so many difficulties and delays we sought a reading with Peter, an English psychic.

We have used Peter's gift from time to time when seeking guidance in our moves. He didn't "see us in Brazil", something we didn't want to hear, especially since we had so much stuff still down there. "Don't let your enthusiasm lead you astray," he told us.

Yet, Peter's visions had always, without exception, been spot on, despite not being what we were hoping to hear. He envisioned us having a "place where people could come to." Peter said he saw us "north of San Francisco." He saw us living with pier access to the water but looking down on it rather than living on it. Well, to say his visions caused us to stop for a moment would be an understatement. We didn't want to believe it. Nobody's perfect. No one is a hundred percent correct, right? Maybe he's wrong this time?

Without the visa we would have to wait six more months before being allowed to re-enter Brazil on a *tourist visa* once again. Our deposit on the fisherman's cottage would be lost and we'd be forced to sell our car, boat and furniture from afar.

Hard as it was for us to accept Peter's reading, all signs pointed toward our having to create Plan B. Through the internet we spoke with Luis and a few other new Brazilian friends and managed to sell all the important items and although we did lose a deposit on the fisherman's cottage, we considered ourselves lucky. Time to get the map out.

Chapter 11

Finding a home

During our time in San Francisco, we were once again invited to the Pacific Northwest, by our old friend Alex Mosalsky. After coming close to wearing out our welcome with Barbara, we accepted his invitation. We had rented a Rent-a-Wreck by the month during our San Francisco stay and flew up to Seattle and did the same. Our previous visit had been from late winter to early spring – it was way too cold for our tropical blood. This was summer, easier to take. We found it to be very comfortable and as beautiful as last time.

For lovers of the water, this area was really impressive. Alex had told us that we'd meet many kindred spirits up in the Canadian Gulf Islands. We drove up there and enjoyed it, but not enough to think of living there. The same held true for our trip to Port Townsend, where many of our Sausalito sailing friends had moved to, during the twenty or so years we were in Mexico and other places. A few friends were building boats, some working in the Boat Building School there as instructors. Others either fished commercially or were somehow in the fish business. All our friends had been able to buy land that they could not afford to buy today. Prices for property had risen dramatically in 20 years. Port Townsend was a wonderful community and one worth our consideration but we had other places to check out before committing ourselves to spend more time there.

When revisiting Panama, while we were waiting for the Brazilian visas, we met James, the brother of a friend, who had come down for a visit. James lived on Orcas Island in the San Juans Islands - between Victoria, B.C. on Vancouver Island, and Seattle. There are Canadian Gulf and American San Juans in the Salish Sea. These island groups are situated in the rain shadow of the Olympic mountain range, and as a result receive less than half the annual rainfall of the City of Seattle.

Park-like, peaceful, very friendly and beautiful beyond belief, we soon were completely drawn to Orcas Island. To explore the possibilities, we rented a room for $400 a month in our friend's house in Eastsound, the main town on Orcas. We bought a rugged old

Mercedes diesel with 250,000 miles on it, and set out exploring every road on Orcas and San Juan Island, its more populated neighbor to the west.

Roche Harbor, a classic resort on the north end of San Juan Island was the home port of another old friend, whom I hadn't seen in some 30 years. Keith was the son of Carl, my former commercial fishing partner and a close friend. One summer, Keith at 15 came out on my boat with Carl and we'd be fishing commercially for crawfish in the Sacramento Delta. The three of us fished for herring and salmon out of Sausalito the rest of the year. Keith loved the fishing life and after Carl's untimely death, he moved his dad's house boat from its berth in Sausalito up to San Juan Island on a boat transport truck. He had purchased five acres of land covered with fir and cedar trees, with money Carl had left him. He plopped the houseboat down on the land to use as his home there. He planted pilings alongside the boat and made it fast to the ground with hawsers, very nautical.

Keith has a fine mind and is handy with tools, wooden boats, construction; you name it and is a graduate of the Wooden Boat Building School in Pt. Townsend. He built a perfect compound in his forest. He cut down the firs needed for constructing another house and barn-like shop and set up his new commercial fishing business. Keith fished for Dungeness crab and Spot Prawns during their seasons. By the time I caught up with him, Keith was considered one of the old timers among the commercial fishermen on San Juan Island. Meeting and seeing him for the first time in ages was like being with Carl, so similar are father and son.

Now that it was like old times, Keith and I picked it up like there hadn't been an absence of three decades. Sitting with Keith on his dad's boat transported me back to the old times, where I'd sat with Carl in Sausalito in the very same seats. Keith filled us in on Island life and the differences in character between the four main islands here; Lopez, San Juan, Shaw, and Orcas.

Another old friend from the sixties in Sausalito, Manya, the former wife of another close fishing and sailing buddy, lived on San Juan as well. Manya is an established artist and jewelry maker who works in silver and has a growing reputation. She ran a bed and breakfast for many years during the high season but these days she spends her time gardening, painting and keeping up with orders for her art through the *Etsy* website. Yes, it was beginning to look like San Juan and Friday Harbor would be a great place for us to give the United States a try again, given that these two pillars of the community would help us with meeting their friends and all. It was a start, it was a sign.

In the end, however, it was Orcas that captured our hearts. We considered it the most beautiful of the islands. Once we discovered Deer Harbor, we were totally hooked. But where could we afford to live?

When we were back in Panama for the second time, while we waited for the Brazilians, I had scanned the web daily for boats for sale in the Seattle area - out of curiosity mainly - but just in case we'd end up in the Pacific Northwest. We noticed the *Sea Wind,* a Spencer 42 sailboat for sale in Anacortes, two hours north of Seattle.

Now that we were in the San Juans looking around we noticed that the boat remained on the market and the price had been reduced. The Spencer was attractively priced so we ferried over to Anacortes and gave the *Sea*

Wind a look. Older, but sound, she was a perfect boat for us at this time. Big enough to sail anywhere and certainly sufficient for the two of us to live on full time.

We made our deal and sailed her over to Deer Harbor with the help of our dear friend Alex. In Deer Harbor we rented a live aboard berth in the funkier of the two marinas. We were set.

Now we had to face closing up in Brazil from afar. Peter the psychic had been correct from the beginning. As he said, "it didn't look like our papers were going to go through". Luckily for us our friend and Brazilian landlord, Luis, promised to help us out and to get the best prices he could for all our possessions there. Imagine the trust. He found buyers for the car and boat. We gave his family the homemaking appliances and bedding we had gathered, even a new bed.

Now after years of thinking we'd never live in the U.S. ever again, we had settled in this very special place. Although the San Juans are part of the U.S., there is a feeling on the island of being almost off the grid. Until recently the electricity would go off at least once in the winter but that is a thing of the past. We love that the islanders tend to be colorful characters and independent spirits; we found Orcas to be fringy enough for our nature and distant enough to feel like we lived outside the US. For the last five years, Orcas has shared a sense of community with us that we have not found anywhere else in our travels.

After living aboard the *Sea Wind* for two years, we moved up the hill from the marina and into our new house. We sold the *Sea Wind* and bought a small runabout power boat. Peter the psychic, proved to be right once again. We can walk down our hill, down a short pier and into our boat. Our home, small and welcoming is plenty big enough for people to come to.

These days we use our little boat to schmooze around these islands, slowly exploring the shores that are home to mink, otters, calico deer and many bald eagles. During the June through September season, we often catch our limits of Dungeness crab. We eat some during the summer and make crab cakes and freeze what's left, to be enjoyed when the snow falls. We still give away most of what we catch to islanders without boats, and find it's a wonderful way to meet our neighbors.

Catching Dungeness crab in these calm, protected waters, between the islands is a fisherman's dream. We are each allowed five keepers a day with each of our two permits during the season in the summer. We use crab traps set at under 100 feet with lots of weighted line and buoyed by a float with our name on it. Our dear friend, Keith filled us in on crab lore including their favorite bait - clams. We live on an island that hosts many types of clam, so at a minus tide, we go clamming. In the beginning of the season our freezer is filled with cockles we have gathered to use as bait in our traps. As the season progresses and the clam cache in the freezer begins to disappear, packages of crab cakes begin to make their presence known, and by the end of the season, it's all crab cakes. Did I say we love it?

We have been accepted in our little hamlet and I have been an officer on the board of directors of the local community club for the last two years. Our club hosts potlucks once a month which they have been doing for at least half a century. These pot lucks are so wonderful that we wish every small town had a potluck to create the feeling of cohesiveness and support that we experience here. For the first time in a long time we are not restless ... well almost. We are talking of exploring Southeast Asia in the coming year but who knows; we've been here for over four years just kicking back...

Life is good.

Chapter 12

Discovery

What did we learn from our travels? How did it change, fulfill, and shape us as individuals and as a couple?

The truest thing was that there is "Power in Intention". Whenever we've put our attention on a project or goal and willed it to become our reality, it usually has or developed into something better. Faith that this was so at least for us gave us strength when we needed it. Also the power of two individuals acting in unison with the same intention is geometric and potent.

In meeting new people, often without the benefit of a mutually understandable language, openness and a smile plus a willingness to communicate and learn from that person or people always won the day. Although some of the mistakes in language resulted in the most bizarre and surreal results, they were almost always crack-up funny.

We learned patience with all people and things and the ability to "Igg", as my dear mother used to say, short for "ignore it." The waiting for our turn at the border or say, an appointment with our lawyer, would go more quickly and be hassle free if we showed outwardly that we weren't going to do anything but humbly wait. Breaking out a book was always a message that that was going to be the case with us. Gringos are so easily riled that we soon came to realize that baiting Gringo tourists to see them explode was an accepted game played by lots of bureaucrats and shop owners in the tourist areas of Mexico. So we learned, just to sit back and wait, saying to ourselves, if this would go like it would in the U.S., we wouldn't be in Mexico!

As people doing business, we had more access to Mexican society than travelers. Being employers automatically gave us some status and when the word got around that we were generous, kind, supportive, and fun, we received a warm respect from the townspeople. Our approach was to share the wealth and as such, we paid our employees much more than the accepted wage. The result of that policy was a crew that valued their jobs and were honest, hardworking, and loyal.

The best thing we felt we left behind was that

the women who worked for us learned to use their minds and make decisions standing on their feet. They also developed job skills like taste, European techniques and the value of creating desserts made with the best ingredients as opposed to the standard practice of cutting corners and using cheap ingredients.

There are many places in the world one can live cheaply while enjoying a high quality of life. We found such places in Mexico, Panama, Trinidad and the Caribbean and know from others that S.E. Asia offers more bang for the buck than most. We got used to hiring help around the house wherever we could afford to do so. These locations offer better and much cheaper health care, transportation and help.

We were fortunate to have started our adventures on a very small sailboat because it was great training on how to do more with less. One of our secrets to success is to keep your overhead as low as possible. We feel this is especially true when thinking of trying out a new business idea. We also think that having less in the way of living space has always suited us and the freedom from unnecessary repairs, cleaning, gardening and upkeep. We have often been floored by the ostentation and waste exhibited by expats who try to duplicate or outdo their dream house specifications in lands where such a dwelling is not only a sign of lunacy but also in a land of poverty says, "We have so much money to waste, come and get it."

From the beginning of our relationship, Teri and I pursued freedom, adventure, and embraced the unknown rather than shape our lives to play it safe and provide for a secure future. That mindset has served us well and although we'd be the first to acknowledge our luck over these years, it's the "We might as well enjoy the ride", as the Grateful Dead remind us, that has been our mantra.

Politics in the U.S. when we left was something neither of us could stand and we were always looking for an alternative to living in the States. Our high standards were almost entirely met in the areas where we've settled.

We value:

Beauty

Clean salt water

Tranquility

Safe place ("no frights here, mon")

Friendly, intelligent People

Open to us

A somewhat stable government.

Favorable economy, i.e. buying power of the dollar

Acceptable and basic medical help available

Laid back atmosphere

That pretty much was and still is our list of requirements for a place to settle. I say settle, because we've stayed and lived for short periods without most of that list and still enjoyed the ride.

Once you've faced the shock and realities of being absolutely broke and have somehow managed to find a solution out of that state, the experience doesn't seem so bad the next time that you're wondering "how am I ever going to get out of this mess?" Confidence in your abilities grows with each experience. We've always taken Deepak Chopra's advice and kept our monies in circulation, never hoarding it. For us, this has worked very well.

We have always known that having or accumulating money does not equate with gaining happiness. Some of the saddest people we've come across have been the wealthiest and we've known why many so-called "poor" people were living and enjoying their lives to the utmost.

We believe that travel is a great teacher as long as one does so with a sense of adventure and leaves the trodden paths of the tourist to understand how the locals live.

There is no power greater than Love.

Enjoy the Ride.

Thanks for reading.

Peace,

Don and Teri

Deer Harbor, Orcas Island
February 14, 2013

About the Authors

The Sailor and the Acupuncturist sailed off together in '87 only to become the co-creators of Mexico's most famous bakery **Pie in the Sky Bakery** of Puerto Vallarta and Bucerias. Both seasoned travelers before meeting, they pursued their risk-taking adventures and entrepreneurial spirits to do what many have dreamed of but never tested.

Flying about the globe and living many years in expat favorites like **Panama, the Caribbean, Mexico, Brazil and Australia** they tried different ways of supporting themselves in each place.

They are married and live without dogs or cats (so they are free to travel on a whim) on a small island north of Seattle, Washington and are avid crabbers.

PIE IN THE SKY ADVENTURES

Made in the USA
Charleston, SC
16 January 2014